"*A Mountain In The Wind* is more than a graceful weaving through the life and spirit of John Denver. It is a verbal passage, an opening into the gentle heart of a poet, a philosopher, a humanitarian, a great soul who entertained the world with his music and mind. He was the evidence of his belief.

Christine Smith's comfort with words and her appreciation of John's earthly mission is reflected in the esoteric understanding of his life and work. John Denver was much more than a singer of songs. His friends knew it and now you can too. *A Mountain In The Wind* is an inspirational must read for all who choose to make a difference."

—Rolland G, Smith

> *(In his 36 years as a professional broadcast journalist, reporter, and producer, nine-time Emmy Award-winning television news anchorman Rolland G. Smith is world renowned for his work. He was also a close friend of John Denver. John Denver said of Rolland, "Rolland Smith is a journalist with integrity. He is a compassionate poet with the spirit of a sage.")*

D1601303

"Christine Smith speaks from the ⅃   ⅃ver, who touched so many lives through his music, his words, and his beliefs. *A Mountain in the Wind* explores the underlying basis of a man who transformed his own passion for a healthy planet in which our children would feel safe into a call for all of us to do what we can to make this a better world for all. John Denver encouraged us to see the world not from our own self-centered perspective, but rather from the wings of an eagle soaring high above the horizon. Christine Smith leads us in understanding this gifted man and provides strength to all of us who are inspired and challenged, like John Denver, to make a difference."

—Dr. Bette Loiselle

> *(Dr. Bette Loiselle is Director of the International Center for Tropical Ecology (ICTE) located at the University of Missouri-St. Louis. The ICTE awarded John Denver the prestigious World Ecology Medal in 1990.)*

A MOUNTAIN IN THE WIND

An Exploration of the Spirituality

of John Denver

By Christine Smith

FINDHORN
Press

British Library Cataloguing-in-Publication Data.
A catalogue record for this book is available from the British Library.

Library of Congress Catalog Card Number: 00-109063

Edited by Lynn Barton
Layout by Pam Bochel
Front cover design by Dale Vermeer
Front cover photograph of John Denver by Inge Kaminski
Back cover photograph of author Christine Smith by Christine Richardson

Printed and bound in Canada

Published by
Findhorn Press

The Park, Findhorn   P.O. Box 13939
Forres IV36 3TY   Tallahassee
Scotland   Florida 32317-3939, USA
Tel 01309 690582   Tel 850 893 2920
Fax 01309 690036   Fax 850 893 3442
                  e-mail info@findhornpress.com
                       findhornpress.com

CONTENTS

DEDICATION

This book is lovingly dedicated to my father and to John.

Father, you provided the loving nurturing I needed to become who I am, capable of doing the things I do—you are part of all I do.

John, my sunshine, you will always inspire me—because of you, I play in the world game.

PROLOGUE

A Letter From John

The following is a letter from John written to you. He had written this letter as his "Message To The Next Civilization" and given it to the World Federalist Association. It is what he most wanted to communicate to those living now and those of a future era, to those who will shape what will happen on Earth in years to come, long after his passing. Courtesy of the WFA, John's letter:

Our civilization has developed to its present perilous condition out of the actions of human beings, not out of uncontrolled vicissitudes of natural forces. Yet we cannot excuse ourselves by claiming ignorance or a lack of understanding. Our failure has not been one of the mind, but rather one of the spirit. It is not what we have not known that has been our downfall; it has been our unwillingness to live our lives out of what we do know.

This is not a philosophical perspective for me but a relatively simple, straightforward conclusion based on my observations of the countless people I have the opportunity to meet. When I watch parents relate to their children, it seems to me that it tells the whole story. We teach our children to develop restraint and judgment, pointing out that it is not wise to use up something all at one time or there will not be any left for later. We tell them it is important not to destroy things they play with, so they will have them to play with later. We develop in them the capacity to share, so what seemed too little becomes enough for all. We observe to them that aggressive solutions to problems are only temporary since they ultimately produce retaliation, and that cooperation lasts forever.

We could not teach our children if we did not in fact know ourselves. Yet, we relate to our world, to our environment and to our resources, as if we did not have the benefit of our own instruction. We interact with each other as if we did not understand that the only thing that works among us is love and understanding.

We justify instructing children by saying they can only relate to what is immediate and obvious. Yet we act as adults as if that is all we ourselves could perceive. As human beings we have the most effective tool of nature; we have a mind that is able to see beyond the obvious, even beyond itself. Still we live as if we were organisms totally controlled by our basest impulses and our most petty thoughts.

For all its history, humanity has lived in the world as if the survival of each of us depended on our getting what we needed and keeping others from having it. It is clear now that the survival of each of us as individuals depends on our sharing with each other. If resources are limited, my survival is assured only to the degree that I provide for you and me, not to the extent that I take for me and mine and deprive you.

This, too, we have in fact always known. We have done ourselves the most damaging disservice by not treating this truth as a simple aspect of reality, but rather as a divine dictum that we could not discover, but only follow.

That which reflects the highest levels of our knowing and the most genuine depths of our loving we have pretended does not exist in ourselves, but must be obtained from an externalized and personified God.

All that is God, all that we need to know to have civilization work is within each of us. We need only be true to what we know and who we are.

Sincerely,

John Denver

FOREWORD

In October 1999, on a Sunday night, my life was changed forever. It was the night I discovered the PBS nature special, *Let This Be A Voice,* hosted by John Denver. It was through John shortly after this, Christine Smith and I met. I believe wholeheartedly that John, in spirit, drew us together. We have become friends, in fact, more like sisters, and have worked together on both the One World John Denver Memorial Peace Cloth and Dreams of Freedom.

Christine writes from Spirit and from her heart. No one can better speak about John's spirituality as evidenced through his music and activism than Christine, who herself is a singer and activist for social justice and the environment. Through her writing, speaking, and activism, and her work with Dreams of Freedom and the Peace Cloth, she has touched the lives of many.

For Christine, like John, is the embodiment of her belief in the oneness of all life. She has dedicated her life to making this world a better place for all who live upon our beautiful Mother Earth.

Through Dreams of Freedom, Christine has seen first hand the impact John Denver's music can have for the transformation of people's lives. Due to her work for Dreams of Freedom and her tributes written for John, she has received hundreds of letters from those whose lives have been significantly affected through the message of his music.

A Mountain In The Wind is an exploration into the spirit of a man who has touched deeply the lives of millions worldwide. John believed in the oneness of all life and he reached out to all through his music. It has been said, and I truly believe, that in listening to John Denver sing, a vibration is felt which reaches deep into the soul and heart of those who are open to the message—the message of peace on Earth, of caring and sharing with each other as a family of man.

With John's tragic death in a plane crash on October 12, 1997, thousands of people worldwide have come together with the sole purpose of carrying on John Denver's legacy, not only sharing his music, but his concern for the environment, the ending of hunger on our planet, and his vision of one world—a world of peace. Millions of trees have been planted worldwide, highways throughout the United States are kept clean, benefit concerts and other fundraisers are held with proceeds going to causes he believed in. All in tribute to a man who gave so much of himself to the world.

John Denver is a candle that lights the way. His message to us is simple: you do what you can do. It can be as simple as picking up the litter you see as you walk along the street, or seeing the beauty of a sunset and sharing it with your child. It doesn't have to be something big, yet if each of us does something every day to reach out to those around us, we are making a difference. It is in this simplicity we can create a better world, a more compassionate and loving world for ourselves and our children.

I once heard a story about John that touched me deeply and I feel it is the very core of what he has come to represent to all of us who love and honor him. In concert, when John sang *The Gift You Are,* he would point to individuals in the audience, saying "You are a gift and you are a gift..." Such a simple gesture and so powerful.

A Mountain in the Wind is an expression of love and gratitude to a man who was not afraid to take a stand for what he believed in. He stood strong throughout his life against all the winds of adversity.

There have been numerous media stories about him since his death; yet none have delved so deeply into his spirit. He was more than a singer and songwriter, he was a communicator, speaking for so many of us not only through his songs, but also in the way he lived his life. To understand the man, we must look at his life closely: Whom did he consider his mentors and teachers? What were his spiritual beliefs? What gave John the strength to continue in the face of his own personal adversities? What books did he read? These are questions I sought the answers to, along with many of you worldwide.

Christine has answered the call and through her book offers us the opportunity to see into the soul and heart of John Denver—through her personal experiences, interviews with those close to him, and her own insight she has given us an opportunity to know the true essence of who John Denver was.

A Mountain in the Wind calls to each of us. It is more than a biography of John Denver; it can also be a blueprint for transformation. I know there are millions of people all over the world whose lives have been transformed by John's music. This book is a call to each of us to go beyond the music and to take the step to incorporate the truth of John's message into our daily lives.

Debra Chilton

June 2000

"I believe that no Divine truth can truly dwell in any heart, without an external testimony in manner, bearing and appearance, that must reach the witness within the heart of the beholder, and bear an unmistakable, though silent, evidence to the eternal principle from which it emanates."

—M.A. Schimmelpenninck (1778–1856)

"A human being is part of the whole, called by us the universe, limited in time and space. He experiences himself, his thoughts and feelings as something separated from the rest—a kind of optical delusion of his consciousness. This delusion is a prison, restricting us to our personal desires and to affection for a few persons close to us. Our task must be to embrace all humanity and the whole of nature in its beauty.

—Albert Einstein

"As you perceive the holy companions who travel with you, you will realize that there is no journey, but only an awakening."

—A Course In Miracles

INTRODUCTION

On October 12, 1997 the world lost one of its most committed peace activists, environmentalists and humanitarians. For many, John Denver was a teacher: a beautiful spirit, much in the way of Buddha, Gandhi, Jesus, Mother Theresa, and other sages over the centuries. All great teachers share a common thread: their belief in unconditional love... and their devotion to putting what they profess into action—regardless of the consequences.

As writer of the international tribute and the worldwide memorials, and as host of celebrations and activities honoring John, I have been blessed to have met some of the most loving individuals ever in my life. These individuals, and the many others who have written me from all across the world, have fervently desired to tell someone of the incredible impact John's music, message, and life had upon their own lives. Many of them have survived excruciating physical and emotional pain and credit John with their pulling through.

My life has been deeply touched by John. I would not be who I am if not for him. That sad day in October brought a pain within my heart I had never experienced. It took months to be able to interact again in strength in the world, and that came only after I realized what had to be done. The truth of John's life, as illustrated in his music and actions, was something I dedicated myself to sharing. Since that decision, I have been blessed to become aware of the miracles which happened and continue to occur because of John Denver. The Spirit worked through John. It always will.

A voice for the children, for the Earth, for humanity—John believed in the unity of all which lives. The spirit of Gaia—the oneness of life—the necessity of each of us choosing to be part of easing pain and suffering, is a fundamental element of his music and his life. The world recognized his achievements by awarding him honors such as the International Center for Tropical Ecology World Ecology Medal, the Albert Schweitzer Music Award, the Presidential World Without Hunger Award, and others.

But the world was also a major source of pain for him. The personal and political repercussions of standing up for truth are great. John endured far more stress and pain than many are aware. It is his courage, through such pain, which speaks to his deep realization of love. He stood for what he believed. He challenged the powerful force of greed wherever he saw it, and this made enemies. Despite the turmoil, he continued to work for that which he believed was true and just.

I write this from my mountain cabin, about a mile from the "crooked Rainbow Trail" (*Thirsty Boots*), where the 14,000-foot peaks surround me, where I wake each morning to deer grazing and hawks and eagles soaring above. As I gaze upon the glistening peaks, I think of John, as I believe he is now soaring, flying as never before. He is free.

But while on Earth he not only flew physically, but metaphorically. He flew where few dare to go: a level of awareness which places unconditional love above all else. For that, he suffered, but experienced too the greatest joy. He was and is a mountain in the wind.

Although his musical career has been covered in the media, his humanitarian and environmental work has for the most part been overlooked or glossed over, and the essence of what drove this man to the selfless compassion his entire life demonstrates has been ignored.

This book, a project I was asked to do by many, is a heartfelt exploration of John's spirituality. It is his spiritual beliefs from which all else came. The lyrics of his ballads, his lifelong commitment to peace, his extraordinary work for Earth and humanity—these are the outward fruits of his quest for truth.

Throughout his life from individuals, books, faiths, and spiritual practices, John developed an understanding of truth and he fervently sought to share that which he came to believe with all who would listen.

Throughout writing this book, I had to quiet my mind and listen to the Spirit. My constant prayer has been essentially, "Not my will, but thine." There are times when a writer, talented as he or she may be in expressing ideas and logically organizing, must put these qualities aside in order to truly communicate what must be said. I have done this daily; sometimes to my own surprise having to completely change or alter a sentence, a passage, or a complete chapter. This work encompasses my own and other's interpretations and life lessons learned from John, but it is something more. It explores the essence of John's life and celebrates it.

I have sought to be a channel for conveying truths I believe he would have us know.

While writing this book, I have taken many walks in these beautiful mountains; smelling the flowers of spring; watching the green of the new leaves; opening myself to the spring and summer rains; resting in my willow chair with sunshine upon my shoulders; all the while— listening.

The 'supernatural' is just a word to help us grasp mentally much in the spiritual realm which is unknown to the physical laws of science. What is often deemed 'supernatural' is anything but beyond the natural. It is of nature—it is of the heart.

This book was written in that way: when I needed guidance and empowerment it came. I pray it will enlighten and inspire. John sang he is with us when the truth is told; I believe you will find him in this text.

John's music shall bless generations to come. His example will inspire others to stand for the things they believe in. But behind the music, the message, the life, it all returns to his heart. There are lessons to be learned there.

It is this I will explore with you—the journey of a man who truly loved.

Peace,

Christine Smith

MY AUTOGRAPH

66 Who I am is in my music," he often said, "I love it when people get that."

Millions "got it" and developed a unique appreciation for John. He was their brother, their confidante, their very best friend. His music transcends time, for it contains universal truths he learned firsthand or studied. Persons of all ages, of many different faiths, occupations, and nationalities, speak of John with warmth. His death brought grieving worldwide.

Despite his popularity as a musician, his life was not that of most entertainers/singers/songwriters. His focus was not the promotion of his craft, but conveying what he was learning and pondering: "I am the songs that I sing."

As he said in a television interview in the early 70's, "I'm consciously working at not taking myself too seriously. I'm not important and I don't want to be. I'm not making a message with my music. I'm simply expressing myself in the avenue that's open to me."

That expression reached millions. His music was his nature expressed in a way each of us could relate to in our own life. Yet, there's something more. It is not just his moving lyrics.

Other people sing John Denver songs, but only when hearing John sing his own compositions is the full significance there. There's a resonance uniquely his, commented upon by many, which reflects his heart; truth is not only in the lyrics, but in his voice and the music itself.

Those who knew John share a common perception of him: that he was exactly who he appeared publicly to be; as he said in a 1979 interview for the *Minneapolis Star* conducted by Jon Bream, "What I want to do is be totally and completely myself and give myself to people."

John was well known for his distaste for signing autographs. He felt it was far more important to look someone in the eyes, hear their expression of appreciation, and relate one-on-one if only for a moment, than to blindly sign a piece of paper.

His autograph is his music—and a life lived in service of "life and the living," as he sings in *Calypso*.

His is a living autograph. Within the mountains, desert, rivers, flowers, wind, sunshine—within the laughs of children, the wisdom of elders and sages—within the music and our hearts his autograph lives.

John believed that despite the grief, suffering, sorrow, pain, there is a purpose. In John's physical death, there was also a purpose. He was an example of what a human being can be. There have been other examples, but if he touched your life, the best honor you can give him is to live your life in unconditional love. John's message to us was that each of us is a gift—a precious gift. No matter what we have or do not have, we can commit our hearts and minds to the things we can do to bless the world. This was his hope for everyone.

As he wrote in a 1986 article (*Windstar Journal*), "We cannot live a lie! We can no longer exist in the contradiction between what we say in our words and deeds as an expression of our fear and separation, and what we hear in the cry of our hearts expressing connectedness and wholeness and the recognition that we are One."

Since John's transition, I have experienced mysterious instances of synchronicity, or "meaningful coincidence": meeting the right person, discovering truly significant friends with whom the bond is as if it had existed for years, finding the answers to my questions or having my needs met through no direct action of my own, experiencing the opening of doors of opportunity and blessing. The common denominator in each instance is its being somehow linked to John.

The world of Spirit interacts with the physical dimension. Where love exists, there is no boundary to what is possible. The love found in his music and life will give us and those after us much to learn from. An autograph which forever speaks of eternal principles and truth is one far more valuable than any ink upon paper.

John said it well in *Autograph*, "This is my autograph, here in the songs that I sing, here in my cry and my laugh, here in the love that I bring."

In an interview coinciding with the *Wildlife Concert* (Sony Music) in 1995, John expressed his recognition that his ability was not solely his own and shared how he wished to be remembered: "I think that I would most like to be remembered for the fact that I stood up for what I believed in; that I spoke for it; I sang for it; I worked for the things that I believe in... in the world."

"I guess the thing I feel best about...I'm not sure that I can say it's what I like best about myself, I don't think in those terms...My music—the songs—the songs that I've written...the gifts that I have, that's why it's hard to say that I like this best about myself. I really don't own this. It is a gift and I'm very grateful for it."

John's deepest desire was to inspire and motivate others to take positive action in this world. He became the catalyst he deeply wanted to be. Because of him, people worldwide have dedicated their lives to humanitarian and environmental work.

John is truly "the love and the light that we all need to see," the best autograph anyone can give.

FRIENDS
FROM OUR HEAVENLY HOME

O ur lives are influenced by economic situations, geography, career choices, physical health, and other external factors often not within our control. The greatest influences – good or bad – are the people who come and go in our lives; this is also beyond our complete control.

We are born into a family which either nurtures or abuses, in a region of the world enjoying economic prosperity or poverty, in a peaceful or a war-torn country. Regardless of the seemingly positive or negative surroundings, it is the people in our lives who can have the greatest impact upon our decision to respond in love or in fear.

Choosing love will not always immediately end the suffering, but ultimately our lives will flower for others and ourselves. Choosing fear leads to hatred, rage, rebellion, anger, and a life of misery.

John was quite candid regarding those in his life whom he credited with helping him choose the path he took. Somehow, through the travels an 'Air Force brat' faces, the perplexities of seeing the hateful prejudice of the deep South, the deep-rooted family heritage he appreciated, the wheat harvests and mill work where he encountered all types of people, the political unrest abroad and in the States–John emerged as a sensitive young man.

He often acknowledged the positive influence of his parent's love upon him, despite the conflicts and misunderstandings that understandably arose between different generations. His love for both his mother and father was strong. He credits his Uncle Dean, for whom he wrote *Matthew*, with opening his eyes and changing his life.

In his autobiography, *Take Me Home,* John wrote, "The world looked great when I was around Dean. I started to get a picture of who I thought I was hiding there inside yearning to come out, and that person was optimistic and positive and upbeat, a happy person who made other people feel good."

That is a description of the man we came to love—and a testament to the influence we can have upon one another.

John experienced those who loved and those who hated; those who were friends and those who were sycophants; those whose expression of goodwill was true and those who beguiled him with falseness. And through it all, he met with some authentic friends from his heavenly home.

Such a friend and mentor was the creative, compassionate futurist Buckminster Fuller, to whom John dedicated the ballad *What One Man Can Do.* Bucky (as he was affectionately called by John) was an outspoken proponent of solutions for world hunger; an inventor of environmentally friendly, resource conserving construction designs; a supporter of renewable energy sources; and an innovator of ways to match human needs with resources. His life's work inspired John, and the two became good friends in their quest to make the world "better than it's ever been before," as John expressed in *World Game,* a song directly inspired by Bucky's approach to engaging people in a personal scrutiny of the resources, trends, and needs of the planet.

John wanted to know, and into his life came the perfect teacher. Simultaneously, John was teaching millions worldwide, sharing, through song, what he had learned.

We are all teachers and all learners. There is no hierarchy among the family of man. John recognized all of us are brothers and sisters. He was, as many people saw firsthand, no respecter of persons. His graciousness and appreciation flowed to those he saw as teachers, just as his appreciation and graciousness flowed to the millions who looked to him.

"A mentor... someone who possesses more experience, spiritual maturity, accumulated wisdom, or a combination of all three than we do," is the beautiful definition given in Kenda Creasy Dean and Ron

Foster's book *The Godfearing Life*. "Typically," they continue, "a mentor fuels our faith journey in intentional and direct ways and helps us discern a faithful life course... Mentors do not use their spiritual maturity as a weapon or as license to create a relationship of superiority. Instead, mentors graciously see their role as fellow travelers and offer appropriate support and guidance."

In Bream's 1979 *Minneapolis Star* article, John acknowledged the role of mentors: "Human beings—we're magnificent creatures. Stuff we do is just incredible. If you see somebody working at such a level of excellence or of personal commitment and wanting to do whatever they do as good as they can possibly do it, God, I want to live up to that... and I want to be an inspiration to other people... If people find meaning to me being myself, or are able to relate to that some way, that's fantastic."

John bestowed the greatest compliment one can give another in his song for Buckminster Fuller when he sang of him: "A friend to all the universe, grandfather of the future, everything that I would like to be." John became that which he admired.

We are not placed here to make it alone. Sometimes a mentor may be a family member; sometimes a friend, in the deepest sense of the word; and sometimes it may be an individual we've never met who speaks to our hearts. In each of our lives there are special individuals whose love serves as an example of the best we can also be. For John, this was Bucky. Others who were mentors and friends for John include David Brower, Al Huang, Joe Henry, and Jacques Cousteau. Such men fall into the category of individuals John described in a 1977 *Playboy* interview with Marcia Seligson, saying, "I don't have any heroes. What I do have is a sense of some people I would like to live up to. They are so real and human, so willing to share themselves that they are an inspiration to me."

For many of us, John was such a mentor. And, in turn, it is we who must be that for someone else.

The lives of those who follow their hearts, in spite of a society which stresses conformity, will contain struggle. The path is not easy. Yes, recognition, as in John's life or as in Fuller's life may eventually come, but only after years of ridicule, economic struggle, and emotional pain. It is hard to stand alone, but if as John sings our spirit and faith is strong, truth will prevail—and at the right time, we will discover the members of our true family.

The feeling of going it alone, the realization of dire suffering in the world, the knowledge of cruelties man inflicts upon fellow man and Earth, and the personal heartaches each of us is subject to, can bring the sensitive soul into the depths of despair. This is a central theme in John's music.

Songs in which he declares this deep sadness are many: sadness for the injustice and horrors of the world, sadness due to personal relationships, sadness for being away from home.

Both John and Buckminster Fuller knew the sadness, despair, and depression that is found in the lives of some of the greatest artists, writers, and thinkers throughout history. At the age of 32, grieving for the death of a child, bankrupt and struggling to support his wife and newborn baby, Buckminster Fuller contemplated suicide at the shores of Lake Michigan. And then, as Fuller explained, the awareness came that his life was not his own, but belonged to the universe and he chose, as he said, to embark upon an "experiment to discover what the little, penniless, unknown individual might be able to do effectively on behalf of all humanity."

Sounds like a description of the visions of a young John Denver, swaying up in a eucalyptus tree, dreaming of being a catalyst for bringing humanity together to work for the betterment of our planet—and Fuller's initial despair is not unlike the despair which had brought John to thoughts of ending it all at certain times in his life.

Yet John remained ever aware of the goodness of life and never lost the realization that there are those who care. One of his deepest hopes was that his life might serve to bring others to the awareness that it is up to them. He emphasized each person is a gift, if only we realized this, we would become a gift to all we meet and in all we do.

Is it worth it? Was a question John pondered in times of despair. Is enduring the forces of darkness targeting you because you have taken a stand for the light worth it? When so many things you've longed for have not come to pass, is it worth still trying? When you're gone, will anyone even remember, much less take it upon themselves to carry on?

We can return to a principle Buckminster Fuller originated: the trimtab—a principle John believed in. A trimtab is a tiny (miniature) rudder located on the edge of a ship's rudder. It's the pressure, small as it is, from the trimtab that pulls the rudder around. So small, seemingly insignificant, yet without it, a great ship weighing tons cannot operate. The trimtab illustrates, as Buckminster Fuller pointed out, the power inherent in the smallest individual part—the power in each of us in this world of magnitude.

"Something hit me very hard once, thinking about what one little man can do... So I said that the little individual can be a trimtab. Society thinks it's going right by you, that it's left you altogether. But if you're doing dynamic things mentally, the fact is that you can just put your foot out like that and the whole big ship of state is going to go. So I said, 'Call me Trimtab,'" Fuller told Barry Farrell in a *Playboy* interview in 1972.

The power of the seemingly insignificant, the power in each individual, became a message John reiterated often.

John believed if you do what you can do, and I do what I can do— together it will make the difference. For only every individual making the choice to do what he or she can will create the sustainable future and healthy environment we dream of.

The World Game, a song written in appreciation for what he learned from Bucky, says it all, "I want to play in the world game; I want to make it better than it's ever been before... I want to make sure everybody knows the score about choosing less... and doing so much more."

There remains within each of our hearts a yearning for true friends, those with whom we can share wholeheartedly and without reserve who we are and what we experience. Such friends are rare. We will not find them by looking for them; they will enter your life when you are completely centered on giving all that you can to whomever and whatever needs the special gift you have to provide.

Those closest to John entered his life as a direct consequence of his environmental and humanitarian work. The universe knows when you are ready for such friends and when they are ready for you. To have a friend for whom you can, with your whole heart, sing *Friends With You* is very precious.

When we dedicate ourselves to love, those friends from our heavenly home come.

A COURSE IN MIRACLES

A *Course In Miracles*, was channeled through Helen Schucman and recorded/transcribed by William Thetford (both Professors of Medical Psychology at Columbia University's College of Physicians and Surgeons in New York City). The Course is an incredible book having a significant impact upon the lives of many—my own as well as John's.

The scribing of the Course took many years. It began when the voice of Jesus told Mrs Schucman, on October 21, 1965, "This is a course in miracles, please take notes." The process was completed seven years later in October 1972. Schucman and Thetford concealed their role in its channeling, with that knowledge only being released following their deaths. The inner dictation and spiritual nature of the text was alien material to both professors; yet both felt they had been selected to communicate a divine message to the world.

The text which has a compelling logic and a captivating, poetic beauty, reflects upon universal spiritual themes.

Many times, listening to John's songs, I hear the Course—a principle I have read here, a phrase or a truth there. Yet, for many years as I studied the Course and as I also listened to John, noting the uncanny similarities, I did not know John too was a student of it.

The wealth of truth so perfectly elucidated in the Course reminds me of what John expressed time and again, principles and ideas such as: "Teach peace to learn it; To have, give all to all; We are the makers of the world we see;" and many others which conjure up the lyrics of so many of his songs. Perhaps the greatest link between the two is in the knowledge that Spirit is working through us.

Just as John said in his *Peace Poem*, "There's a name for war and killing, when you know another answer, for me the name is sin"; the Course also defines "sin" as lack of love. Focusing again on the truth, the answer lies always in love.

A Course in Miracles teaches us to have just a "little willingness" to the Spirit—to its workings and to its purpose—and from there miracles of understanding occur for us and thereby for others. John had that willingness, and miracles happened. Healing, both physically, emotionally, and spiritually has happened and continues to happen worldwide because of John—because of the Spirit working through him, which John himself frequently alluded to in interviews throughout the years. He realized there was a power, not of his own, which worked through him.

The Course says miracles are only necessary because of the darkness of perception in the world; thus, miracle workers are here to teach and heal. The eight special principles of miracle workers describe John's perception of the world and his existence in it. The eighth principle states, "You can do much on behalf of your own healing and that of others if, in a situation calling for your help, you think of it this way: *I am here only to be truly helpful. I am here to represent Him Who sent me. I do not have to worry about what to say or what to do, because He Who sent me will direct me. I am content to be wherever He wishes, knowing He goes there with me. I will be healed as I let Him teach me to heal.*"

That is our mission, it was John's mission: to live one's life in service to all, allowing the Spirit to work miracles through us—going where it leads.

Only after John's transition, did I learn that for many years John read the Course. What a revelation and happiness that has brought. In the foreword to Gerald Jampolsky's book *Good-bye To Guilt*, John wrote, "I, too, am a student of *A Course in Miracles*... [It] tells us that 'you cannot change your mind by changing your behavior... but that you can change your mind.' And when someone truly changes his mind, 'he has changed the most powerful device that was ever given him for change.'"

I have been told by those close to John, he often spoke of there being but two emotions: love and fear. This is one of the most fundamental teachings found in the Course, with chapters examining how all the injustices and wrongs of the world stem from fear—and how love is always the answer.

Love is "such a mystery," we find John saying in an early song, *Till You Opened My Eyes*. Later in *Perhaps Love* he wrote of the many different ways people think about love, and then, many years on, in the *Wandering Soul*, we find the wisdom and the maturity of understanding his entire life had shown him. "Suddenly the mystery is clearer, That love is only letting go of fear...Love is the answer, and love is the way, Love is knowing just what to do and what to say."

John learned love isn't something "out there" to find or make happen: it's already there within each soul, as it is the essence of each human being.

The Course teaches that only by recognizing the divine within every other human being, can we recognize the divine within ourselves, and only then can we really love in the truest sense.

All are equal; all are one. The Course speaks of some people thinking of themselves as "special," their egos telling them they are better, superior to, more deserving than others, and it teaches us that only through relinquishment of the ego can we get back to recognizing we are all the same—and that only then do we experience love.

This theme occurs throughout John's most beautiful songs—*World Game, It's About Time, Let Us Begin, Wandering Soul, It's A Possibility*, and numerous others. In *Raven's Child*, he sings of the great injustices which occur when fear does the choosing between right and wrong, and emphasizes the need for each and every one of us to recognize "the source of our sorrow and shame... we are one." We must understand that the capacity for good and evil lies within each heart and recognize that the essence of every human being is divine. Only then can we love all truly, knowing that those who choose differently may be in darkness, but are none the less our brothers and sisters. We are one.

Other truths from the Course, such as "Giving is receiving," and "Love is extension," are found in John's songs. In *Heart to Heart*, he sings, "I know that love is everywhere, always safe, always true, and exactly where it comes from is where it's going to." Again and again, this message is found in the Course—"the answer to suffering we see is as simple as you and me."

Dr. Thetford was once asked his definition of the Course, and replied, "To help us change our minds about who we are and what God is, and to help us let go, through forgiveness, our belief in the reality of our separation from God. Learning how to forgive ourselves and others is really the fundamental teaching of the Course. The Course teaches us how to know ourselves and how to unlearn all of those things which interfere with our recognition of who we are and always have been."

That was John's constant desire in life, to know himself, to know others, to know forgiveness—to know love.

The Course examines how we confuse ourselves with past thoughts, allowing our minds to bring us agitation. Through the main text, the workbook for teachers, and the manual for teachers, it conveys insight into the central cause of all the problems on Earth: the ego. Although usually regarded as healthy, the ego, in truth, is responsible for our belief in differences, giving the illusion that each of us is separate from the other, when in reality we are one family.

In a world full of judgment, deceit, intolerance, and anger, the Course is a breath of fresh air, giving us the mental and spiritual ability to clear away the false and emerge as the true person we are. The purpose: To create a world of peace. The way: Allowing the Holy Spirit to guide us.

A quote from the Course: "Peace now belongs here, because a Thought of God has entered. What else but a Thought of God turns hell to Heaven merely by being what it is? The earth bows down before its gracious Presence, and it leans down in answer, to raise it up again. Now is the question different. It is no longer, 'Can peace be possible in this world?' but instead, 'Is it not impossible that peace be absent here?'"

The Course teaches us how to attain inner peace first, then proceeds to instruct us how to become peacemakers in this world. John's life exemplifies many of the teachings of the Course.

For myself, in times of confusion, I have put one of John's CDs on, only to find the perfect message I needed. I have done the same with A *Course In Miracles*, opening it randomly for an answer—which is always there. All those who apprehend deep truth in John's songs, will also discover it in the Course. Like John's music, in every reading (or listening) we learn something new, we remember a Truth that was always there, but which we had forgotten. Therein is awakening.

DREAMS

Dreams, John knew, are the substance from which all wonderful creations and accomplishments emanate. Yet, we live in a society which does all it can to crush them, categorizing them as fanciful and unrealistic. To dream is enlightened–to pursue the dream takes courage.

In his music John dreamed of the way it could be. He knew the power of dreams as a boy. He kept the understanding of their importance throughout his life.

One of his first dreams envisioned a place where people came from all over to explore ways to make the world a better place. In a 1986 *Parade* interview with Lisa Birnbach, John explained, "I was about 12, in Tucson. And I used to get up in this very tall tree, and I would sit there and think about things. I had a vision that one day I would have a place in the mountains, and I'd have friends who would come from all over the world to visit this place. I thought I might be a catalyst for their being there, and friendships would grow out of that. That's a pretty mystic thought for a 12-year old kid."

In a 1991 interview, he spoke of even earlier dreams, "Once, when I was about 9, I was lying in the backyard in Oklahoma, looking up at the stars. All of a sudden, I finally felt connected to something."

He dreamed of harmony, and as he explained in his autobiography, Take Me Home, he was perplexed why other children and adults fought over differences. He dreamed of things being different, and was ridiculed for not being a fighter. But John was a fighter, only he used a superior force: love.

Although he studied architecture in college, he dreamed of pursuing his music. To pursue such a dream was considered frivolous, but pursue it he did. Summers spent on wheat harvests or logging in the Snoqualmie National Forest in Washington state found him practicing his music every possible chance. In a 1972 interview with the *Seattle Times,* John told with irony how a logger added to his desire for an appreciative audience, "He got annoyed at my singing and hit me with my guitar. Knocked me out. Didn't hurt the guitar."

"Nothing was happening in Texas [where he was studying architecture] with the exception of the music and nothing else really worked for me," he told Chett Flippo in a 1975 *Rolling Stone* interview; "The one thing I really decided to do as good as I could and learn and grow with, was the music I did."

Soon, thereafter, John, age 20, made the decision to try to make his dream of singing for those who'd like to listen a reality. Professors, family, and friends all told him he was making a big mistake. And in a beautiful act of love, despite their reservations, his parents gave him hard-earned money from their savings so John could head out to California to do what he felt he must.

Some people would call it luck, but John's career breaks prove a powerful spiritual point. When we venture out for a dream from deep within, forces are at work to aid us: seemingly coincidental happenings, such as meeting the right person in a most unlikely spot; learning of an audition; linking with others from whom we'll learn. Each of our lives, like John's, are filled with these unusual happenings when we are following our hearts.

In a 1974 interview with *TV Guide* reporter JR Young, John spoke of the dream behind his music, saying that everything happening for him was, "a fantasy from 10 years ago when I was sitting on a life-guard tower in Long Beach, California, and ached to sing to people. I dreamed about it. I wanted to do what I felt I could do, do it so well that there would be more people than we could handle. And I'll tell you how hard I dreamed. I dreamed just hard enough to make it real. Now it is, and I love it."

Synchronicity (meaningful coincidence) is seen in John's life through numerous instances he shared in his autobiography. The common denominator of each occurrence was that he had the courage to try, regardless of probability, regardless of what others thought. John realized dreams are far more than mental conjuring or imagination, and that pursuing them opens a pathway for mystical happenings to help us fulfill our dreams.

In a 1988 interview for the Australian *New Age News,* he told reporter John Esam, "You do have the opportunity to fulfill everything you aspire to in this life. The Universe, or God, or the Spirit, or the Whole, however you want to say it, is there to help you fulfill yourself on this planet."

As the great German philosopher and poet, Goethe, stated, "Whatever you can do, or dream you can, begin it. Boldness has genius, power and magic in it."

Yet, somehow on life's path, occurrences we at one time dreamed of may seem blocked or unattainable. In *Rhymes and Reasons,* John sings of "the dreams that have escaped you," with such sadness, for he understood the burden and heaviness of heart we experience when dreams are unfulfilled—or not even explored. For while we may not always realize our initial dream, to have tried is essential to the human spirit. To complacently resign ourselves to the mundane is to give up who we truly are.

As he sings in *Higher Ground,* regarding those who do not follow their hearts "... [they] are giving up their lives for something that is less than it can be."

John's pursuit of his of being a singer/songwriter resulted in the lives of millions being blessed. When such dreams live within our hearts they must be followed if our lives are to fulfill the purpose we were put here for. John never stopped realizing this and his dreams grew bigger—from the personal to the global.

"Given the possibility of living up to the dream in me, you know that I'll be reaching for higher ground," he sang, and he exemplified each word. The higher ground John sought consisted not only of his personal dreams of living where he needed to be and doing what he needed to do, but of dreams for all humanity and the Earth.

Early on, John felt a connection and inspiration from nature. As with anything he cherished, here dreams were formed—dreams of a sustainable future for which he worked, using environmental activism, education, political means, and his music. Yet though the dream of Earth being protected is a grand one, it was, he emphasized, attainable, if each of us did our part. He wrote, "There are so many things that need to be done that sometimes it seems overwhelming. I try to remind everyone that no one person has to do it all, but if each one of us follows our heart and his own inclinations, we will find the small things we can do. Together we will come up with enough to create a sustainable future and a healthy environment."

Two individuals John admired deeply were the activists Olaus and Margaret (Mardy) Murie. They exemplified all he believed in, inspiring him to pursue both his dreams for the Earth—and his dream of true love. It is for them he wrote the beautiful *Song For All Lovers*.

After Olaus' death, John wrote in his essay, "In the Quickening Light," that Margaret "continued to work tirelessly on behalf of the dreams they shared. One of those dreams was to help protect Alaska's wilderness... she did." In his 1995 *Wildlife Concert* he reiterated his admiration for Mardy, saying she had done more for the wilderness of Alaska than any other human being.

Mardy and John visited only two months prior to his death, and the love between them was like that of a mother and son, I have been told.

From the Muries' example, John learned lessons, as he wrote in "In the Quickening Light": "While I yearn personally to experience this kind of love between a man and a woman, such a capacity for love offers important lessons of many kinds. [One of those lessons is] that it teaches us to believe in our dreams because they will come true, even as we remember never to take them for granted... It transforms promise into principle, curiosity into commitment."

John realized many dreams in his life and yet there were those which remained. In a July 1997 interview with the *Potomac News,* he said,

"There are a lot of things I would like yet to do... I feel like in every aspect of my life, I'm still growing."

The greatest dream John had he would not see come to pass in his time on Earth. In one of the sweetest songs he ever wrote, *A Baby Just Like You*, we find John wishing his child the gift of a world where "peace on Earth fills up your time, that brotherhood surrounds you, that you may know the warmth of love and wrap it all around you... It's just a wish, a dream I'm told from days when I was young."

John died in a world of greed, destruction, and killing—a world where people devote their lives to exterminating other races and faiths, where governments kill their own citizens in the name of justice, where retribution reigns and money is the measure, where there's enough food for all but where many starve, where money turns hearts to stone, where forests and oceans are destroyed to increase bank accounts—a world which pained him deeply.

In *Let Us Begin* John challenges us, "If peace is our vision, let us begin." It lies with each of us to make that dream, which has occupied human hearts for generations, a reality.

BLESSED ARE THE PEACEMAKERS

"Blessed are the peacemakers, for they shall see God," Jesus proclaimed in the Sermon on the Mount.

John's fervent desire to see the world at peace is evident both in his music and his activities. In 1984 when cultural exchanges were resumed between the U.S. and the USSR, John was one of the first American artists to perform in the Soviet Union. In 1987 he returned to hold a benefit concert for the victims of Chernobyl.

In 1992 he performed in mainland China and was the first western artist to perform in Vietnam, after the Vietnam war.

He helped to found the Hunger Project; was appointed to President Carter's Commission on World and Domestic Hunger, and as a member of its fact-finding delegation toured drought and starvation-suffering nations throughout Africa. He furthered cultural exchanges and performed numerous benefits for causes benefiting children and the environment—and these are but a few of the more well-known actions he undertook.

Peace, John knew, is not only the absence of war. Peace is far greater. Peace is a world for everyone. No sorrow. No hunger. No injustice. No greed. Peace is a world without political or racial boundaries. Peace is an existence where love reigns in one world.

John dedicated his life to this vision; consequently he was persecuted by opposed to his message. Every peacemaker in history has met with this.

People in darkness, those who value their ego agenda, whatever form it may take, are enraged when light shines upon their darkness. And as anyone living in the mountains knows, one single candlelight can be seen for miles in the darkness. Light has great power to illumine vast darkness. John spoke his mind. If he saw corporate greed as responsible for a terrible affront upon the environment, he identified it. If he saw national priorities putting politics above the welfare of those in need, he spoke out. But those in darkness are angered when their motives are revealed for what they are. They defend themselves and strike out in anger.

But truth needs no defense.

Peacemakers throughout history are both beloved and hated. Although many treasure their messages, there are always others who react in anger, even to the point of killing the peacemaker.

John was persecuted by many. His candid willingness to share his beliefs and spirituality was met with all manner of boycotts. Certain fundamentalists viewed him as a threat. John spoke of unconditional love, while they spoke of conditional love. Termed "new age" by such religious groups, John and his activities were said to be part of an "anti-Christ" plan. John's devotion to making this one world is still a concept many oppose.

By boycotting *Oh, God,* and *Rocky Mountain High,* by threatening John's life for his extensive work to save the Alaskan wilderness or for his openness in sharing his spiritual beliefs, by attacking his character, by misrepresenting events in his life with innuendo or sarcasm, those in opposition to John's message attempted to stop him and today continue to relentlessly attack who he was.

There is an onslaught of negative media coverage regarding John—a strange occurrence considering the media usually forget deceased individuals whom they regard merely as entertainers. Yet, in John's case, negative television stories, as well as negative articles in print publications, continue. What is it they fear?

It is those who live after the death of a peacemaker who continue the dream. Consider how the lives of Martin Luther King Jr., Mahatma Gandhi, and other teachers of loving unity continue to inspire us. As John sings in *Relatively Speaking,* "The living need the dead."

There are many ways of being a peacemaker. It's in all we do each and every day. For some of us it may be politics, for others, teaching, environmental work, or humanitarian projects. For some, it's not the career we're in, it's the way we treat people in our daily lives. It's the attitude and behaviors we harbor toward our family and friends, the strangers we encounter, the criminal in society, those of differing belief systems, and even those who hate us.

As John told a reporter in the early 70's (as quoted in James M. Martin's *Rocky Mountain Wonder Boy*), "People on an individual basis will make changes, not protestors or lobbyists. People who do what they really know to be right or true. Little things. In traffic, in grocery stores, you let somebody else in front of you. That's peace. You have to have some consideration for the things around you and the things that happen. Then, there's joy, great joy in life."

Another key trait John exemplified is the ability to empathize. Empathy is not mindlessly jumping on the bandwagon of a social cause because it's the in-thing to do. It is being involved because our hearts feel others' suffering as if it were our own. In spirit, all suffering upon this planet is our own.

When John sings of hunger, it's not in the abstract. When he sings of the dead, the burned, and the dying, it's not an imaginary scenario. When he sings of the hunted creature slaughtered by human whim, it's not as a shallow, casual observer upset at the death of an animal.

It is from the perspective of those who suffer: not from the mind of a westerner in a rich country, but from the depths of the heart of a "global citizen," as he referred to himself—a concept we must all adopt. Though John loved his country and gave breathtaking renditions of its national anthem at numerous public events, (he was celebrating the freedom and way of life enjoyed by its citizens), he was not placing his country and its citizens above others, but recognizing the goodness which he wished all people to have. Ridding ourselves of nationalism is the first step toward world unity. It's not "us" and "them". It's comprehending, as he says in *Children of the Universe*, "that life is more than always choosing sides."

Peacemakers share this: No one entity—be it nation, race, species, religion, or any other distinction—holds their allegiance. Yes, they may be placed here to work for the freedom from bondage for a particular people or country, but their lives will show love for all, for they know love can never be divided.

This is the battle we're all in: endeavoring to be good human beings, who are tolerant, compassionate, and actively expressing love as much as we can. It's up to each of us to do this, despite the pressures of the world telling us otherwise.

We must diligently examine every aspect of our lives—placing love as the priority. Peacemakers do not merely give lip service to the things they say they believe, they do something about them.

"Peace is a conscious choice," John told the *Minneapolis Star and Tribune* in November 1983, "I have great confidence in people to make a choice when the options are clear. Part of what I'm doing through my music is putting the new options out there."

His commitment to peace is best seen when he sings. There are times when his eyes flood with tears: for these are not just poetic words to him, he feels every word of which he sings. When John sings *Wake Up, Jimmy Newman*, he becomes the soldier watching the sun rise, smelling the breakfast, watching the attractive nurse—all the while calling his friend to wake up to this new day—the day, he calls to Jimmy, we're going home. Wake up—wake up—and as the crescendo is reached, John is the soldier crying out in agony. His friend is dead.

Songs such as *I Want To Live* and *It's About Time* demonstrate the same emotional commitment. In singing these ballads he truly becomes the song. But singing of peace was simply one expression of his dedication.

He hoped the United States would serve as an example for other nations. In the essay, "Let Us Begin" (published in the *Windstar Journal*), John spoke of his visit to the Piskaryovka Cemetery where 470,000 Soviets who died during the 900 day siege of Leningrad are buried in graves marked only by the years 1941, 1942, or 1943, graves with weeping mothers, graves which inspired John to write the song and essay "Let Us Begin". In this powerful essay, John questions why we continue spending billions on the war machine when so many are hungry, when couples cannot afford to have children, when family farms are being lost. Is this peace? Is this even trying?

Oh, God, the hugely successful film in which John and George Burns starred, was chosen by John not just for its humor but for the nuggets of truth it contained. As John explained in his lecture at the International Center for Tropical Ecology in 1990, one particular scene made John want to do the movie—the scene where the character Jerry Landers speaks to God in the shower room: "Jerry's talking to God and asking him why God chose this particular time to make an appearance. And God says, 'Well, I made the world to work.' And Jerry says, 'Well, have you read the papers lately, cause it ain't working.' I felt that way then as I feel it to a large degree now. And Jerry asks God, 'Why don't you do something about it?' So, God says to Jerry, 'Why don't you?! It's your world.' Well, I have always felt that if we're going to deal sufficiently with the problems that confront us, no matter who we are; where we live; what our color is; what the expression of our faith is, it's not going to come from some divine intervention. It's going to be out of our own actions. And, Jerry says to God, 'But we need help,' and God says, 'That's why I gave you each other.'"

"Peace," John said in his "Let Us Begin" essay, "is a conscious choice. It is time for all of us to begin to invest with every ounce of energy, with all our resources, with every breath we take—in life."

As *A Course In Miracles* states, "It is through *us* that peace will come."

EST

John sought freedom throughout his life. I shall never forget watching John, who was then about 30, singing *I Wish I Knew How It Would Feel To Be Free* on the BBC's *Shepherds Bush Green Show*. Though he didn't write that song, the sincere feeling with which he sang it was obvious. His dream was to know what freedom really felt like and for all to be free.

Around this same time, John found Erhard Seminar Training–EST (and Latin for 'it is')–and began to experience freedom. For "it is" is about taking responsibility for our own lives.

A look at some of its fundamental teachings can show us why est appealed to John and how it influenced his music. Because of the enlightenment John felt he obtained in his est training, he dedicated the *Farewell Andromeda* album "for all of you from Werner and est and me," and he wrote and dedicated *Looking For Space* on the *Windsong* album to "Werner Erhard and everyone in est". *Looking For Space,* I believe from my own life and from the many testimonials of people worldwide, may have affected more people than any other of his songs; yet few know that est was the inspiration behind it. As often happened, John's willingness to share his spiritual awakenings and transformation brought awakening to millions.

Many years ago, I became interested in est due to my knowledge of John's high regard for it. Though I never took the seminar training, I read extensively and find the principles true to this day. *Looking for Space* has and always will be a song which defines my life; studying the inspiration John received to write this song is enlightening.

Est began and grew to its height in popularity during the 1970's, and as such found its way to Aspen, Colorado. Bringing a whole new way of looking at our lives, challenging societal preconceived notions of why we are here, and destroying the concept of a personal identity of emotions, belief and intellect—est focused on the idea that we are the creator and source of our experience.

Founded in 1971 by Werner Erhard, who became a friend of John's, it was based on Erhard's personal transformation, which had mystically occurred out of the blue as he drove through traffic on his way to work; "What happened had no form. It was timeless, unbounded, ineffable, beyond language... I realized that I was not my emotions or thoughts. I was not my ideas, my intellect, my perceptions, my beliefs. I was not what I did or accomplished or achieved. Or hadn't achieved. I was not what I had done right or what I had done wrong. I was not what I had been labeled—by myself or others. All of these identifications cut me off from experience, from living."

Erhard's incredible awakening was something he had to share. He had discovered freedom in the midst of this chaotic world—and that, as we know, was something John yearned to discover for himself.

Erhard continues (in *The Book of Enlightened Masters: Western Teachers in Eastern Traditions*), "I was simply the space, the creator, the source of all that stuff. I experienced Self as Self in a direct and unmediated way. I didn't just experience Self, *I became Self.*" Erhard saw his life from an entirely new context; "It was an unmistakable recognition that I was, am, and always will be the source of my experience."

Like John, Erhard had spent years studying spiritual practices of the East, yet for any such influences, est has a basis all its own. As John said in his autobiography, *Take Me Home,* "est is about being honest, about working through to an expression of your real self," and "Space was a metaphor for what needed to be internalized. It wasn't a fixed entity, but spiritual territory to be staked out and built upon... Before est came into the picture, I was already searching for expressions of myself, beyond my music, but it was est that gave me the confidence to follow through."

The seminars consisted of two days of intensive self-exploration in which participants were guided through a training freeing themselves from emotions and attitudes holding them back. The training brought people face to face with the false identities they accepted as who they were, and once discovered, provided them a way to eradicate the illusions from their life. Though est became quite controversial, many of those like John who completed the training, had nothing but praise for the awakening it brought to their lives.

I would liken the apparent strong physical and emotional experiences people underwent during the sessions to the reactions experienced when going through de-tox for any harmful substance in the body: there may be serious withdrawal symptoms as the physical poison is released from the body—and in est it would seem the body reacted to the release of emotional poisons previously stored within the heart and mind.

Listening to *Farewell Andromeda*, the title track of the album he dedicated to Erhard, we hear and sense the liberation of which John sings and the responsibility he takes for the creation of each and every day of his life, two primary principles learned in est.

The happiness he sang of was shared by thousands who experienced est seminars, for opening spaces of personal growth and breaking the binding chains of memories, regrets, and other negative experiences was exactly what many needed then, and now. It was here John realized expectations of him were unfounded, childhood hurts need haunt him no longer, and the world was unlimited—what he dreamed of doing was within his control—giving him an inner courage to do all he later accomplished. His past shyness and reluctance to speak out were overcome. It was all his choice. Or as he sings in *Love Is Everywhere*, "Life is the fruit of your own creation."

Est taught people to put their pasts and their limiting belief systems behind them; it gave them an opportunity to start with a clean slate, so to speak. You are in this moment—in this space. What are you going to do with it? It freed people from their false identities, identities based upon society, their peers, their family, and upon limiting negative emotions and self perceptions. It said here's the day—the moment—you make it what it is. As Erhard wrote, "Create your future from your future not your past."

Est's fundamental principles freed John to reach a potential he never knew possible, and taught him how to get to a space of no regrets. (As he declared in the 1995 *Amazon*, "let this be a voice of no regret." To have no regret means each of us realizes the state of life as we know it is precisely our creation: all we see is our responsibility, the culmination of all our dreams and visions.

If people are starving and hurting—if forests and skies are polluted—if suffering is happening—it is the responsibility of each of us to halt such injustice. Each individual is making a difference, either easing suffering or causing it. Our very existence affects the world. The only question is whether ours is a life of apathy (part of the problem) or destruction, or a life in which we choose to create goodness.

Some counter such a notion by saying it's the responsibility of world leaders, but John disagreed. One of his most eloquent explanations of personal versus political responsibility came in his prelude to singing *I Want To Live* at the 1981 concert in the Apollo Victoria Theater in London, when he said regarding world hunger, "Some 15 to 20 million people starve to death every year on a planet that truly has more than enough to go around. It was the determination of our commission [President Carter's Commission on World and Domestic Hunger] after two years of study that we really do have the where-with-all to eliminate hunger on this planet forever... and ever... that it need not exist. Our commission's report said all that's missing is the political will to do something about it. I disagree with them a little bit. I think that what's required is the *popular* will, and that when it becomes the *will* and the *voice* of the *people... that* will make it political... and we can see an end to this obscenity in our lives."

This speaks of John's belief in individual responsibility, and reflects his passionate devotion to ending hunger—yet another need that he and Werner Erhard would tackle together in the formation of the Hunger Project. Founded by several, including John, Erhard, and Buckminster Fuller, the Hunger Project commits itself to this philosophy of taking responsibility for the world around us, most specifically for hunger.

Although est seminars ended in 1984, the legacy est gave us lives on in the lives of thousands who grasped their potential to make a difference in the world. It is part of the philosophy behind the Hunger Project that continues today to educate people in the reality of ending hunger, if only humankind commits itself to it.

Apollo Theatre, London
October 1982

Arnhem, Netherlands,
19 May 1990

Mannheim, Germany, 19 May 1986

John receiving the
International Center for
Tropical Ecology
"World Ecology Medal"
13 September 1990

© Inge Kaminski

Frankfurt, Germany,
May 1992

© Inge Kaminski

Frankfurt, Germany, May 1992

Frankfurt, Germany,
8 November 1992

Windstar brunch, Aspen,
Colorado, 25 August 1995

Topeka Kansas
Performing Arts Center,
12 August 1995

© Inge Kaminski

Frankfurt,
Germany,
19 May 1992

Windstar Symposium,
Aspen, Colorado, 26 August 1995

© Inge Kaminski

Windstar brunch, Aspen,
Colorado, 25 August 1995

Press Conference,
Frankfurt, Germany,
9 October 1995

Frankfurt, Germany,
9 October 1995

Nürnberg, Germany,
16 October 1995

Windstar Symposium,
Aspen, Colorado, 26 August 1995

Gent, Belgium,
5 November 1995

Ludwigshafen, Germany,
20 October 1995

Royal Albert Hall, London,
19 March 1997

Royal Albert Hall, London,
21 March 1997

Jesse Jones Hall
for the Performing Arts,
Houston, Texas,
26 September 1997

Houston, Texas,
27 September 1997

LIFE AND DEATH

John was not afraid to die. Neither was he afraid to live.

There is no fear of death among those who believe in love, for an inner understanding is reached that, "Living and dying are both your most intimate friends." (*We Don't Live Here No More*)

Death is not an ending; it is merely a transition from one existence to another. It's simply leaving the body behind while the spirit flies. Many "live" their lives so concerned with the security and protection of their bodies, they never truly experience life. Life isn't about protecting ourselves to such a degree that we fear doing things and experiencing challenges which might result in physical harm. We are so much more than our body; it is but a vessel, a shell, a vehicle meant to be used to do the good we can while we are here in this form.

Millions think they are their bodies, and thus they spend years providing for and protecting themselves; all the while they die little by little each day, never reaching the heights they were meant to reach. But as John sings in *Eagles and Horses*, "My body is merely the shell of my soul, but the flesh must be given its due."

John loved life. He celebrated it. The thought of losing his life in the pursuit of what he loved doing never stopped him. He knew how to truly live—not merely exist. While in the flesh, he was determined to experience life to the fullest.

Here are a few of the things he savored: knowing the goodness of being away from it all, he would backpack and camp in remote mountains—from the Rocky Mountains of Colorado to the peaks of the Himalayas in Tibet. He fished lakes throughout the world, he loved boating and rafting, gliding, mountain climbing, photography, painting and drawing, horseback riding, motorcycling, golfing, snow-shoeing, traveling to remote and dangerous areas of the world for the benefit of others, writing, cooking, studying the heavens, and, of course, flying. Yes, we might be criticized or threatened (as he was) for writing and speaking for the environment; yes, we might be injured or die in pursuit of a wondrous remote camping trip in the wilderness or perhaps in an airplane crash—but that is unimportant. To live means to experience whatever our hearts lead us to do; to deny ourselves such experiences is to deny life for fear of death.

John loved flying helicopters, jets, small private planes, experimental aircraft, and gliders. Tom Poberezny, President of the Experimental Aircraft Association, of which John was an active participant and supporter for over twenty years, says of John's passion for aerobatics: "I don't think he did it with the idea of being serious about it as much as just enjoying the exhilaration and the feeling it brought."

Some of the happiest smiles seen on his face are when he's walking toward his plane, or when he's flying, or even when he's engaged in another activity and he hears that buzz of a small plane. A good example of this occurred in September 1990 when John was being presented with the International Center for Tropical Ecology's World Ecology Medal. He delivered one of his most eloquent speeches on his vision for the Earth and what fulfilling this vision would take for each of us—all the while interrupting himself whenever small planes or jets came over. He couldn't resist showing his happiness as he looked skyward, a huge smile upon his face, saying "I'd like to be flying one of those!"

He often said there was nothing more relaxing than flying. Frequently questioned by interviewers regarding its risk, he gave an answer to Ray Martin that summed up his feelings: "You take a risk when you get up in the morning... you take a risk crossing the street, certainly to get on an airplane and fly halfway around the world to do an interview. I feel much better when I'm in control, quite honestly, and I feel a lot more comfortable out there. Yeah, there's a risk; so you take care of your engine, you're responsible for your airplane, you know what you're doing, you know what your parameters are." And then after a breathtaking flight in which John took Ray on a ride in his Christen Eagle, falling out of the sky between the Maroon Bells in a hammerhead stall, John said enthusiastically, "I don't know how to have more fun that that!"

The *Challenger* disaster (John had been tentatively scheduled to be aboard that very flight), did not cause him to lose his desire to go into space. Speaking to a Senate subcommittee regarding space exploration just two months after the *Challenger* tragedy (as reported by Lisa Birnbach in *Parade Magazine*, August 17, 1986), John said "I feel responsible as the catalyst for the Civilian in Space Program. Until President Reagan said the first civilian should be a teacher, I believed that was my flight. If I were to go up in the shuttle—and not as an entertainer, not as an educator, not as a journalist, but as 'Everyman,' as a world citizen—I think it would get some notice. It would be a real shot in the arm for a lot of young people about the future."

And as far as fear of death? He continued, "I tell you today, I would have been proud to go—and in retrospect, too. It's a risk to get up in the morning. I would go tomorrow."

Ralph Waldo Emerson wrote "As soon as there is life there is danger." John lived this truth. Death is not our enemy; fearing death is.

As we find in *Tao Te Ching* (D.C. Lau translation), an ancient spiritual text credited to Lao-Tzu—and much loved by John, "When going one way means life and going the other means death, three in ten will be comrades of life, three in ten will be comrades of death, and there are those who value life and as a result move into the realm of death, and these also number three in ten. Why is this so? Because they have set too much store by life. I have heard it said that one who excels in safeguarding his own life does not meet with rhinoceros or tiger when travelling on land nor is he touched by weapons when charging into an army. There is nowhere for the rhinoceros to pitch its horn; there is nowhere for the tiger to place its claws; there is nowhere for the weapon to lodge its blade. Why is this so? Because for him there is no realm of death."

As found in Luke, "Whosoever shall seek to save his life shall lose it; and whosoever shall lose his life shall preserve it." Protecting the body by keeping themselves from perceived risks, at the expense of neglecting fulfillment of their hearts' convictions, is a terrible tragedy many choose.

There is a time we are born and a time we die. Nobody on Earth knows what comes before or after, although many claim to know. It is stated in the *Tao Te Ching*, "Those who know do not speak; those who speak do not know." Not that those with wisdom and knowledge don't share with others, but it is often the ones who know the least who make the most noise. True wisdom begins at the point we can say "I do not know," for there is the beginning of all understanding. Or, again from the Tao, "To know yet to think that one does not know is best; Not to know yet to think that one knows will lead to difficulty."

Disregarding those who claim to blindly know based purely on a set of dogma they have been taught, there are those with a knowledge this world does not recognize. It's not scientific, it's not religious. As the saying goes, "The heart has reasons the mind knows nothing of." It is this form of reasoning and knowing which is far more conducive to apprehending what the reality is.

In *On The Wings of a Dream,* a song inspired by the death of his father, John ponders death: why are we here and so soon gone—what is this life? Here we find the truth, "we are more than we seem." He sings of the gift given each of us, the life we have and the lives who are part of ours. The most powerful message here is, "though the body in passing must leave us," we must listen to the voices within and realize we are never alone.

From his earliest years, John was not satisfied with pat theological answers. Questions arose within him when he heard teachings inconsistent with love from those purporting to teach love.

Even as a child, John identified hypocrisy, as he shares in his autobiography. Having been brought up in the church where he studied the catechism and sang in the choir (which he loved), at around the age of twelve he became uncomfortable with attending and he was "suddenly turned off organized religion," although some things remained from which he spiritually grew. As he shared in *Take Me Home,* his catechism teacher "broke faith" with him when the teacher put on a false show of being upset as a way of reprimanding young children for something they had done. An incident followed which exemplified John's seeking for truth and his knowledge that nothing is beyond questioning. When another student asked a question about a parable being studied, the teacher became dogmatic, indicating the children were not to question it—just to accept it. And as John wrote, "I wouldn't buy that. Twelve-year old kids have built-in radar for the sanctimonious. It didn't make sense to me that there would be anything that you couldn't question." Fortunately, John maintained such questioning throughout his lifetime, and thereby came to a knowledge and communion with Spirit deeper than most. But his appreciation for those hymns remained, and many years later in 1994, he spoke of *How Great Thou Art* as being both his and his mother's favorite hymn.

John expressed belief in a force beyond which we comprehend—'God' if you will. In an interview conducted by Dan McLean for BBC Radio in 1994, John delved, though lightly, into these beliefs. McLean began with: "I interviewed Sir Bernard Lovell recently, and he said to me 'The more you investigate the universe, the more you believe in the existence of God.' Would you agree with him on that?" To which John said, "Yes, I would," continuing later in the interview with, "there is obviously some intelligence governing all of this. Something beyond our abilities seemingly to comprehend. And, I think, you know in our desire to understand ourselves, to know ourselves, is really to find where we come from and where it is we may be going."

John clearly believed in our existence prior to being born unto Earth and in our continued existence thereafter, for as he stated in *Take Me Home*, "I believe that light is where we come from and where we go to."

He found truth through a variety of spiritual teachings and traditions, seeing that each one has love as its guiding light and provides unique insights into how we can implement and manifest love in our lives. The references are unmistakable in his songs, many of which are essentially prayers. In *Falling Leaves (For the Refugees),* he praises and exclaims that his heart is filled with love for the precious day and the gifts he has been given. In *World Game* he sings praises to God, exclaiming emphatically the Hebrew prayer, *"Yaweh, Yaweh, Yaweh Jah."* His regard for the best of the Christian faith is apparent in *It's About Time:* "There's a light in the Vatican window, for all the world to see, and a voice cries in the wilderness, sometimes he speaks for me, I suppose I love him most of all when he kneels to kiss the land, with his lips upon our Mother's breast, he makes his strongest stand." Again in *Rhymes and Reasons* we find a prayer for those who don't believe in love, and his heartfelt renditions of *Potter's Wheel, Let It Be,* and *Gospel Changes* convey his appreciation for a message he strongly believed.

"The true king sits on a heavenly throne, never away, nor above or apart," a king, John sings, who rules with wisdom, mercy, constant compassion and who lives in the love within us (*Raven's Child*).

Often referring to the higher power, a creator, or the universe in both the masculine and feminine, John used the terms of indigenous peoples from North America, Australia, and the Arctic, singing of "Our Father watches over us, our Mother will provide," in *It Amazes Me* and in other songs like *Trail of Tears* and *African Sunrise.* For he understood that the reality of 'God' does not belong to one belief system; it lives within each of our hearts, regardless of our particular faith, solely if we believe in love.

As quoted in James M. Martin's *Rocky Mountain Wonder Boy,* John once remarked in the early 1970's, "My closest belief in the Creator is what the Indians called 'The Great Spirit,'" an understandable concept for John to relate to since he too found his communion with the wind, the sky, the water, the lands.

The song I am most questioned about is the powerfully moving and poignant *The Wings That Fly Us Home.* No song expresses John's feelings upon life and death more clearly. Written with his friend and co-writer Joe Henry, it perfectly communicates both the mystery of what is to come and his apprehension of it. We have lived before—we live now—and thereafter we will be fully conscious of the ones we love who remain. A very special song to John and Joe, John's essence lives within its verse and music. It speaks truly of the bond of love—a bond death does not end.

John is both the mountain in the wind and the prophet in the meadow. Now that he has made the transition, it is the vision of his goodness which must sustain us through the cold.

Reincarnation—John read about it widely, and numerous references to it appear in his songs, references to knowledge from ancestors, from the universal memory, and, yes, even from a knowing beyond what our current lifetime has taught us: the wisdom of the prophets and sages, the memories of a home never seen before. John experienced looking into a baby's eyes and seeing such wisdom and sureness that he could easily believe the child had lived before.

Yet, such knowledge, he knew, also comes to us in our daily lives. Was it precognition or the fulfillment of what he already knew would be part of his life, when he envisioned the mission to see Windstar realized, or when he dreamed precisely how his adopted son would look?

John did not permit the mystery to occupy his thoughts to the point of distraction. While parts of the truth and answers may come to our hearts, many questions yet remain. It is a mistake to preoccupy ourselves with that which is a mystery. We must simply ponder and accept that we do not know. There begins the knowing.

John was a student of Buddhism. Though he never presumed to refer to himself as Buddhist, he lived the life of a modern sage. In *What the Buddha Taught* by Walpola Rahula:

> The Buddha was asked, what things shall one not reflect upon? In response, Bhikkus (the Buddha) stated reflecting unwisely on these things give rise to confusion, only hindering one's growth: 1. Did I exist in the past? 2. Did I not exist in the past? 3. What was I in the past? 4. How was I in the past? 5. Having been what, did I become what in the past? 6. Shall I exist in future? 8. What shall I be in future? 9. How shall I be in future? 10. Having been what, shall I become what in the future? Or, now at the present time he is doubtful about himself: 11. Am I? 12. Am I not? 13. What am I? 14. How am I? 15. Whence came this person? 16. Whither he will go?

Those questions arose in John, as they arise in any contemplative spirit. But there comes an understanding that we must not focus upon these notions at the expense of living what we know to be true today. Speculation is natural, but preoccupation with that which we may not be meant to know at this time is detrimental to the mission we now have in this lifetime.

To ever state we 'know' anything because it has been written or told us by a text or person is fallible. True 'knowing' comes from the soul within, not from anything outside ourselves. John used tools (books, 'holy' texts, teachers, music, spiritual practices, etc.) to further his understanding. He was receptive to learning truth wherever it may be found. Yet to believe anything required confirmation from the Spirit itself—the voice which speaks to us if our hearts are open, our minds are quiet, and we are still. As Emerson wrote, "Belief consists in accepting the affirmations of the soul; unbelief is denying them."

As John sings in *Sweet Surrender,* despite the wondering, "Right now it seems to be more than enough, to just be here today." And though both the 'past' and 'future' are unknown, Spirit is there to guide us. If we follow only that light we will realize "life is worth the living;" we don't need to see the end. When and if we are to know of elements of mystery, it will be told us, as it was to John. If we simply surrender to living life fully now, all else will come in good time. We must just be.

So for those who wonder in what existence is John now, and shall he return again, I offer my conjecture: He is free. He is flying—soaring. Whether he will return as a human being again, I do not know. My personal belief is best stated in an essay entitled "Universal Love" from Buddha Metta-sutta's teaching (Walpola Rahula translation/*What The Buddha Taught*), "Let one's thoughts of boundless love pervade the whole world—above, below and across—without any obstruction, without any hatred, without any enmity. Whether one stands, walks, sits or lies down, as long as one is awake, one should maintain this mindfulness." For a person of such insight, which I regard John as being, "Verily such a man does not return to enter a womb again."

Steve Rafferty, a man whom John helped raise funds for disabled athletes in Great Britain, wrote a piece called "Memories" in which he related his last meeting, in March 1997, with John. Rafferty wrote, "I was interested to learn that he [John] firmly believed that when he passed from this earth to the next, that his spirit would be lifted and taken *On The Wings of an Eagle* to his spiritual home high above the Rocky Mountains."

John's off-the-cuff remark, spoken softly as he hangs high from a vertical canyon wall on a small ledge overlooking a golden eaglet's nest, in the beautiful documentary *Let This Be A Voice,* reflects his love—and desire—and perhaps his knowing, "This is what I go for when I'm flying... seeing the world like this. I want to be an eagle. If I come back I'll be an eagle. You can count on it."

I'm a Human Being

" See, here's the thing, I'm a human being, you know," John said in response to Ray Martin's excellent interview with him, as they discussed the deep emotional turmoil John experienced.

In direct proportion to the exceptionally wonderful high John derived from singing before an audience of 20,000, he also experienced what he called periods of incredible depression.

He went through the struggle we all go through, with the additional difficulties and stress of having his personal life in the public eye at all times. He was put in the position of having to determine people's true motives: Are they there for me because they care—or simply because of who I am?

The media, for the most part, treated John harshly. Anything that showed he was less than perfect—they headlined. So it is with those in darkness. Enemies of virtue seize upon anything to attack those in the light; yet those in truth realize all make mistakes, all are fallible human beings.

John did not want to be considered special. He did not want to be put on a pedestal, though he realized many put him there. When he made mistakes or did things some might perceive as wrong, his greatest concern was that public knowledge of them might hinder someone's ability or receptivity to listening and learning from his music. He was acutely aware that celebrities are seemingly expected to be perfect and that when they are not, they are ridiculed and accused of hypocrisy. John knew that what he sang was truth. At the same time, he was aware he made, and would make mistakes. Overcoming his fear and realizing that sharing intimately was essential, John candidly exposed much of his life in his autobiography.

As he said in a 1994 *E! Magazine* interview, "As I think happens to a lot of people in showbusiness, you get put up in a pedestal. And I think the thing that comes out in the book is that I'm a human being."

As a young man, shy and lacking worldly knowledge, he pursued the ache within to sing. The songs he initially sang, those he wrote and the ones he chose to sing, reflect, for the most part, the love within his heart. He, of course, engaged in entertaining and performed light, irreverent songs of humor as well, but even in the earliest performances and tapes, when he sang music of substance he shone. Songs which meant the most to him he sang with the greatest passion; his voice (even in his early years) reached its full potential and magic when conveying what he so dearly wanted to share.

While some took, and continue to take, glee in exploiting his foibles, his obvious humanity reached the hearts of millions. For despite mistakes, despite the pain and sorrow, despite the hardness of life we all go through, John remained committed to the things in which he believed. When he erred, he was the first to admit it. What separates him from most is that he took such diligent care to learn from those mistakes, endeavoring not to repeat them—both to ease the pain he suffered as a consequence—and to avoid causing pain to another. And he shared those experiences through song.

The pressures around him led to the mistakes—in relationships, in business, in the way he conducted himself. These are the things many choose to focus upon: the strife of failed marriages; the drinking; the anger; the depression—to me, such experiences point so much more to the strength and courage he had. While many disintegrate under such duress, he maintained his sense of purpose.

"I'm a human being, you know. I'd love to be the world's greatest guy and I'm not. I'm a pretty good guy. I've been a pretty good father. I made a bunch of mistakes; and I've learned a great deal. I've gone through some difficult times," he explained to Ray Martin.

Some regard him as a saint, and some as "God among us," but John would have us know he was but a man. If we perceive "God" in him it is because he chose to follow the divinity found in each of us. The Bible says in 1 John 4:7: "For love is of God; and every one that loveth is born of God, and knoweth God."

He lived the divinity within him, and that is something few do, but it is possible for all. He was our brother, as were those who came before him such as Jesus, a man here on Earth showing us the potential we can achieve—a brother who lives amongst us, teaching, and experiencing all we too experience. Though such men or women are enlightened, the power of their existence comes from the realization they are just like us—they live and learn—sing and cry.

His personal losses touched us. People sympathized with John when he divorced twice. The death of his father brought condolences from all over the world. He shared his soul through his music and people responded.

Such transparent honesty is rare.

At some of the darkest times in his life, depression enveloped him and he considered suicide. The depths of his heart he spilled in songs such as To The Wild Country, Eclipse, All of my Memories, Looking for Space, How Can I Leave You Again, Seasons of the Heart, Thought of You, On The Wings of a Dream, and A Wild Heart Looking For Home.

John experienced all emotion deeply. He was an artist, and, as with other notable artists throughout history, his sensitivity enabled him to create works which reached millions, while simultaneously feeling the joys and pains deep within. He shared his vulnerabilities with us, thereby developing our trust and concern for his life.

As John sang in Spring, "Yet as different as we are, we're still the same." It was the point he most wanted us to grasp. We can live our lives, as he did, blessing humanity and Earth—if only we choose. We must do what we can, regardless of our own personal hardship.

John gained much wisdom through introspection. Following the release of Dreamland Express, in an E-Tonight segment, he spoke of his father's death, his divorce from Annie, and of his apparent 'new image', expressing sides of himself never before revealed: "All of these things have had a very profound effect on my life... and I think in the process of it I've not been destroyed—I've not stopped—I've more than survived, I've matured... This old body here has got a few more dents. It's covered quite a few more miles than it had 10-15-20 years ago. My heart is still the same."

The reason many feel so close to John is that he annunciated the feelings so many of us experience but never share. The happiness in life we are more apt to discuss, but often in the darkest moments of our lives we close up. Others may try to comfort us, if they are even aware of the inner suffering—but there remains beneath our outer appearance submerged hurts, fears, memories, and deep sorrows.

In a 1977 interview with Peer J. Oppenheimer for *Family Weekly*, John said, "I feel there is truth in my music—truth presented in a way that has no restrictions on it. I would like to be a catalyst. I would like my life to be so true and so honest a reflection of me that people see themselves... Music is far more than just entertainment. It's a tool for coping."

It was impossible to know his music and not know him. In essence, from afar, we came to know this man to a much greater degree than we know many of those in our lives.

Known for taking himself seriously, he delighted those around him when his playful side showed itself. He enjoyed playing practical jokes on friends, and had a few played on him. His laughter and smile were genuine, and evoke people's fondest memories of him. He spoke easily to strangers, taking time to truly relate to who they were in the few moments they might share together. He was open and candid, and not afraid to express naiveté about things he did not know, even laughing at himself as in his account of a youthful trip to New York City where he struggled to find words to say to a beautiful woman he saw as he strolled the city streets. As she gazed into a store window, young John dressed in sandals and jeans, asked if she is was model. To his embarrassment, she replied, "No, I'm full scale." This incident wasn't his only humorous encounter with models. As an English lady told me, in 1972 John met her and was curious as to what models kept in their cases. So she opened hers, and John found to his amusement vanishing cream. "Does it really make things vanish?" he asked, laughing as only he could. When she explained it was used under face powder as she used no foundation, he said, "Well, you're pretty enough without it." Such charm and willingness to engage in conversations with all remained with him always. John related to all equally.

Kris O'Connor, John's friend and tour manager for over 30 years, describes John as "pretty much happy all the time," and says that the image the public had of John was "pretty much the same" as the man himself. "I thought people considered John a lightweight, but I thought he was kind of a heavyweight. One of the early articles... was John Seagraves' first review of John as a solo, with the headline 'Anybody Who Would Badmouth John Denver Would Kick A Puppydog.' I sort of always believed that. He meant what he said and he stuck to it."

One of O'Connor's fondest memories is "Going fishing with John. Watching his face light up when he'd catch a fish and no one else had caught one yet." Having fished with John in Alaska and New Zealand, he recalls an incident in Lake Taupo, New Zealand, "We had bets with the other boat. John, being so competitive, didn't like to lose at anything. We found about a 28"–30" dead rainbow trout on the bottom of about 15 feet of water and we snagged it. Rigor mortis had set in so it looked sort of like a half moon. We tied it onto our line and as we were trolling in we made it jump out of the water. Thought we had the guys. We laughed and laughed and laughed."

O'Connor describes John as tired after concerts; "He put everything into it. We did one tour back in the 70's. It was 63–64 shows in 50 some days. Vietnam and China were the roughest."

However he might be feeling, he endeavored to be honest and giving with those who appreciated him. Even while undergoing extreme personal difficulties, he did his best to relate to those he met with warmth.

He knew anger throughout his life, though he was one reluctant to express it. The incident that received the greatest media coverage was really one of the least important in his life and is commonly misrepresented. When his wife had a stand of scrub oak he loved cut down and he chainsawed their dining room table and bed headboard, the event was sensationalized worldwide. He explained to Ray Martin what had caused him to react: "I asked her why she cut the trees down... They were as much a part of the home as the walls, and the floor, and the roof; and how could she do that without talking to me about it? And she started wagging her finger at me..."

Who cannot understand the feelings of a man who designed his home—and had scrub oak he adored, which took years to grow, where he could look upon them from his window—a man who designed his home in relation to that beloved greenery—who came home to find his wife has had a stand of them destroyed?

As he told the British *Daily Mail,* "The day I planned that house, I went to the site with the builders, and I said: 'I want an imaginary line through the main room to run straight through those two sets of scrub oak trees and those mountains out there.'"

Far beyond that outrage, John's righteous indignation showed itself in his battles on behalf of the environment. The toughest being his outspoken outrage at the Exxon *Valdez* environmental disaster. John made no attempt to hide his disgust at the tragedy or the greed he believed responsible for it.

As John said on a 1990 Geraldo show especially for Earth Day's twentieth anniversary, "I get angry. I was never more angry in my life than I was on the shore of Prince William Sound," as he continued to explain the incident need not have happened.

It was when he discussed such experiences as visiting the Prince River shoreline or walking in the world's greatest, most poverty-stricken slum in India or hearing the last cries of a baby dying from starvation in a remote African village, or seeing the destructive infringement of humankind upon pristine wilderness in Alaska or visiting the graves of millions who have died in war—that we see his deepest anger—an anger which never remained simply that, but always became a call for action.

John sought to remind us of the things we already know within our hearts and to stimulate us to see what it is we can do for this world. The important thing being—he did this selflessly. He used his celebrity status as a platform, but sought no praise for doing so. This is precisely why his legacy will continue.

As the *Tao* says, "Evolved Individuals put themselves last, and yet they are first. Put themselves outside, and yet they remain... Evolved Individuals lead others by opening their minds, Reinforcing their centers, Relaxing their desires, Strengthening their characters... [they] are a part of All Things and overlook nothing, They produce but do not possess, Act without expectation, Succeed without taking credit... Is it not because they are without self-interest that their interest succeeds?"

As John once remarked, much to the criticism of the unenlightened, "I am God," which he explained is the truth for every human being, not for himself alone. He said it in the sense of appreciating the divine within himself, and he emphasized the need for all to recognize that the divine is in each of us and throughout the universe.

His commitment to love was there as a boy, as a young man, and at the height of his success; through grueling emotional life situations, his heart remained the same.

MUSIC MAKES PICTURES

John's music, full of metaphors, speaks to the heart and mind, touching our emotions with its deep understanding of love, challenging us to become part of the movement to ease pain and suffering.

Try as others may to sing John's songs, the total power of his compositions lies not in the lyrical and musical notation alone—but in his singing of them. Though others may do a good rendition, the power we feel when John sings them is absent.

His songs address the essence of our lives: hopes, aspirations, dreams; first love, unrequited love, loss of love; life transitions as we mature; struggle, loneliness, despair, and sadness; happiness, humor, joy, and celebration; politics, nationalism, war; nature and wilderness; beliefs; questioning; inspiration; life and death itself.

His was not a performance, but an attempt to communicate to us, his listeners, what he felt. His songs were sung from the heart, thereby reaching the heart. Whatever emotion or situation a song expressed, he became it in that moment. The truth of his songs is in every word and note and in his entire countenance. As the poetry of his song engulfs us, he, the channel, is engulfed as well.

He was an exception in the world of music, poetry, and art. As the late Joseph Campbell remarked in a New Dimension's interview with Michael Toms (collected in the book *An Open Life*) regarding the woeful lack of poets who speak of the mystery, "It's the work of poets and artists to know what the world image of today is, and to render it as the old seers did theirs. The prophets rendered it as a manifestation of the transcendent principle... today... I think poets and artists who speak of the mystery are rare... opening of the mystery dimension–has been, with few great exceptions, forgotten. I think that what we lack, really, isn't science but poetry that reveals what the heart is ready to recognize."

"Poetry that reveals what the heart is ready to recognize..." an excellent observation applicable to the miraculous communication of truth millions find in John's music.

His songs of praise for the wilderness were inspired by the beauty he found there, and by his deep desire that others come to know nature's wisdom through his songs if not by personal experience. He wrote in the LP accompaniment to *Windsong,* "I hope that at some time in your life, you'll be able to go someplace where it's quiet, where there are no cars, no dogs barking, no planes passing overhead, and that you will be able to listen to all of the music that she gives us. If you're really lucky, you'll be able to sit by a lake at the foot of a mountain and hear a storm come and go. There is beautiful, beautiful music there. All you have to do is listen." All could get a sense of what he sings of in *Let The Mountains Talk, Let The Rivers Run,* "There is wisdom there... much to learn... much to know... much to understand."

John felt he was singing his best in the last several years of his life, and, indeed, his voice took on a far richer depth, which lent itself perfectly to the serious nature of many of his songs. It became quite apparent that his voice only improved with age... a rarity for singers.

When young, we can express our longings, hopes, and sadness, but we do not yet have the experience in such matters that a lifetime of joys and sorrows brings. In time, we discover what it truly means to love and what it truly means to despair. Thus, those songs written early in his career took on a greater meaning for him, and when he subsequently sang them, a newfound quality–the richness of a wisdom gained through many more experiences–could be heard.

As he said in a July 1997 interview with Beau Yarbrough for the *Potomac News,* "I think I'm singing better than I ever have before. I'm starting to learn how to sing... I think the songs are as good if not better than they ever have been before," or as he expressed to *Currant's* rock critic, Roger Catlin, in 1995, "I'm pleased to show the difference in the way I'm singing now than the way I was singing 15 years ago."

The lyrics themselves are poetry. Try reading them—it brings clarity and understanding, as there is so much that can be missed. The lyrics can stand alone, because John was a fine poet and quite deserving of the Colorado Poet Laureate award bestowed upon him by Governor John Vanderhoof. He was also a multi-talented, multi-faceted musician, capable of playing many instruments exceptionally well; this made his musical compositions and his playing extremely captivating. His many instruments included the harmonica, which he combined in a virtuoso performance with his singing and guitar playing. Added to this was his ability to sing a number of songs or verses as in *Annie's Song* in German, French, Russian, Japanese, Spanish, and even Mandarin and Gaelic.

His music brought images of a life where there is goodness, friendship, and hope for a better tomorrow; as well as touched our souls with the darkness which surrounds us; yet even in the saddest of songs John conveyed a subtle vision of the way it could be—if we try. The meaning of his verses becomes more apparent as we experience more in our own lives. No matter at what stage of life we are, there are songs that precisely convey the very thing we feel.

As John explained to reporter Tim Cooper in 1994, "What made me the biggest selling record artist in the world is that people hear my songs and say 'That's how I feel, too.' I have this gift and when I talk about things like global community and a possibility of creating a better world, maybe these things too will light a little fire in people's hearts and bring to the fore more activities and demonstrate that. Hopefully, some of that will get through. That is what I do all this for."

His songs, from his earliest compositions to his latest, mean so much to people they have been played at weddings; during births; by a surgeon when he operates; for those making the transition from this life to the hereafter; and for funerals, fulfilling the requests of the deceased.

His musical compositions for the album *Sunshine* (soundtrack for the 1973 CBS made-for-TV film based on a true story of a young woman's struggle with terminal cancer) and his other songs were of such a comfort to the dying woman (the subject of the film) that she had *Take Me Home Country Roads* played at her funeral.

It was when John sang alone with no backup and no band that the purity of his voice and passion of his emotion is most apparent. The live performances where he sings with only light accompaniment communicate a greater depth than the concerts or recordings with a full band. For though the accompaniment makes for richness and is most enjoyable, to a degree it prevents us from hearing his voice in its completeness, particularly on several of his most heartfelt ballads.

With or without backup, there's a special quality to viewing John as he sings, an element which only adds to his power to reach our hearts. To see his joy as he sings *Rocky Mountain High*, or the tears he's holding back in *I Want To Live,* for example, touch us whether we are watching him in person or on video. Similarly, when John sings by a river with mountains rising behind him, or around a campfire, or anywhere in the outdoors where he truly feels at home, he gives his best and most joyful performances.

His songs featuring powerful political/social commentary continue to inspire people to become involved in issues they've never thought of. He expressed his support of the civil rights movement; his opposition to the Vietnam War (although he supported its returning veterans); his abhorrence of the war machine, hunger, and all forms of inhumanity; his disgust at greed and its effects on people's lives and our precious Earth; his empathy with the homeless, the prisoner, and the hurting. He parodied governmental and social groups who believe themselves superior. No topic was off limits in his music. Even when John recorded songs radically digressing from his usual style, such as *Hold On To Me, The Chosen Ones,* and *Chained To The Wheel* (by Australia's Joe Camilleri), his choice reflected his concern for the plight of those who struggle.

To define is to limit—so it is in attempting to examine John's music. My heart is filled with knowing which defies my ability to adequately express it in words.

Thus, Pat Cavanaugh, a John Denver issues activist, was asked to write the following critique. Her appreciation for John is strong, and yet she is able to analyze his music objectively, providing another viewpoint and valuable insight into John's music.

A Critique of the Music
by Pat Cavanaugh

Soaring like an eagle, swooping like a hawk, John Denver's voice carried its listeners on a wave of exquisite beauty, sometimes resonating from the mountaintops, other times, whispering softly as an alpine flower. By his voice, and by his music, he induced people to appreciate the wonders of nature, to experience the agonies and ecstasies of love, to be concerned about the plight of hungry children, and to understand the need for peace.

As a young man, he sang in a pure, crystalline voice that was so sweet and fragile it seemed it would break at any moment, yet that moment never came. Instead, the voice grew stronger and in the process even more beautiful. In the 70's, he adopted a powerful, high-pitched, yet slightly nasal vocal style which served him well, as that was the period of his greatest popularity. However, a musician with perfect pitch, Denver could not long be satisfied with that sound, so he undertook training to improve his delivery. In addition, he obviously worked hard to make his voice an instrument that could almost move mountains and change the course of streams. His 80's voice retained the crystal purity of his early years, yet a dimension was added, a richness and depth which effectively created an earnest, seeking style. He needed this style for such songs as *It's About Time, What Are We Making Weapons For?* and *Amazon (Let This Be A Voice)*.

In the 90's, Denver's voice took on yet another mode, that of a mature, deeper-voiced, more masculine man. There was a hint of a catch in his throat from time to time which added to the emotional impact of his music a greater resonance and a richer fullness. Yet, with all these changes, he never lost the purity, the perfect intonation, and the amazing range.

The *tessitura*, or range, exhibited in his voice was so significant that in the space of six months in 1996, two major newspapers, the *LA Times* and *Washington Post* respectively, in reviewing his concerts, referred to his voice as "soaring tenor" and "burnished baritone." It's no doubt possible for many men to sing in both ranges, but John did so very effectively that listeners to just one song would swear he was one or the other, not both. True, the very highest notes of the tenor or the deepest of the baritone eluded him (though further training could well have brought them forth), but what was there was exquisite, never strained. In his later years, Denver did adjust the keys in a few songs to make them more comfortable. From time to time, his voice failed him, because of exhaustion or illness, yet he forged onward, almost never letting an audience down. He could complete a two-hour concert, singing with a sore throat and fever, and apologize for having "sounded like a frog." Yet, the audience never guessed anything was wrong.

There was power in his voice. One Scottish fan was amazed John could "still belt 'em out." He could indeed. Frequently, in the last concert on a tour, John would be so exhausted it was seemingly difficult for him to walk onto the stage, yet his singing would bear no hint of weariness. Even if his voice cracked, as it was prone to do in later years, the notes between the cracks were so fine, rich and sweet that the cracks were immediately forgotten. Yet, because he was a perfectionist, John worried over such slight mistakes, often apologizing to his audience. There was, in addition, a certain thrill in listening to him perform live. John never totally controlled his voice—or controlled the emotions that were always close to the surface for him—so an audience was never sure when he would have a problem. Problems, though, were relative, and in John's case, never detracted from the overall beauty of his music and voice.

As far as musicianship is concerned, the very fact that John Denver songs from more than 30 years ago are still being played on the radio, sung around campfires, performed at weddings, and even used in movies proves that he was a true musician, not simply a songwriter. The term "songwriter" seems to imply a person who puts some words together, strums a few notes, and hence... a song! Even a Denver song written in ten minutes, as he always claimed *Annie's Song* was, has a tight construction, a plan into which every part fits neatly. Some critics have criticized Denver for "sparse" lyrics, but if one examines his songs closely, one can easily see that there is no need for more complex lyrics, because everything that needs to be said has been said, and in such a metaphorical style that the desired aim is achieved.

If he's writing about newfound love, the joy and promise sparkle in the lyrics and melody, as in *For You*. If the opposite is true, and love has ended, the melody and words echo the ache in the man's heart (*Seasons of the Heart*). No writer/singer has ever examined the many facets of a man/woman relationship as thoroughly and exquisitely as John Denver did. *Whispering Jesse* is a perfect example of an aspect of love quite possibly unique to him. The song examines the nostalgia of an old man remembering his long-dead lover and the simple pleasures of their life together. Now, he's alone—in a nursing home—but his memories bring him a measure of joy.

This heart-felt quality of John Denver's music is equally true of his "teaching" songs. When he wrote and performed *Amazon*, audiences everywhere vowed to do whatever they could to save the earth's precious environment. Even when he performed songs written by others, Denver made them his own by his warm, exact and beautiful interpretations. *Whalebones and Crosses* was written for John by Lee Holdridge, his arranger, and lyricist Joe Henry. When he sang it, it came from his heart. So open and strong was that heart that these two people close to Denver were able to capture exactly what he wanted to say in the way he wanted to say it. *American Child* is another example of a perfect *menage à trois* of music, lyrics and voice. The passion with which John sings that song is perfectly matched to the emotional and evocative lyrics (by Henry) and melody (by Denver).

In fact, another unusual aspect of the songs he wrote both the lyrics and melody for is that the music always blended so perfectly with the lyrics that the listener knows it could be no other way. This technique made some of his music easy to sing, as audiences everywhere will attest.

Whether it be a relatively simple song such as *Annie's Song* or a complex one like *Rocky Mountain High*, audiences everywhere joined in—often at John's urging. This is not to say the songs can easily be sung well. They are clearly more beautiful when sung in John's voice, but they could be sung by almost anyone. Possibly some might say this is a negative—that his music was too simple—but that's not the case; the fact is that John's unique talent created music that was accessible on one level, yet difficult on many other levels.

John Denver's "spiritual" songs are among his best. His was an ever-questioning mind and heart, and his questions and the answers he sometimes found are expressed in relatively simple words and beautiful melodies. *It Amazes Me* is a powerful song of the wonderment a human feels in the face of the unknowable, and Denver's lifting melody provides a counterpoint that effectively carries the listener into his space. *Looking for Space*, in fact, is a slightly earlier song which has almost the same effect. To the very end of his life, John Denver was actively seeking "the answers to all of my questions," and perhaps he found some of them, as he seemed to be more at peace then than at any point in the previous 15 years.

No one seems to know how to categorize John Denver's music, and that may be part of the problem with his popularity. Self-appointed critics of popular music have been tempted through most of his career to ridicule the lyrics as maudlin, saccharine, optimistic. Well, they were sometimes all of the above, but mostly they were not. Even one of his most overtly optimistic songs, *Sunshine On My Shoulders*, is not all that optimistic; the verses are written in the subjunctive mood: "If I had a song that I could sing for you..." implies that he does not but wishes he did. Of course, the overall theme of the song is as optimistic as sunshine, but what on earth is wrong with optimism? Some may consider certain of his love songs overly sentimental, such as *For You*, yet it effectively captures the feelings any human being has upon first falling in love and the melody is perfectly designed to display John's thrilling tenor.

Most of Denver's songs are multi-layered. Listeners can enjoy them simply as beautiful melodies with pleasant, evocative words, or they can examine what those lyrics are actually saying, and find deeper meanings, meanings which vary with each individual's experiences and dreams.

In essence, John Denver combined the best of folk, country and popular music into a totally unique style. From folk, he used the themes of political protest, as in *I Want To Live*. From country, he borrowed the themes of country and family and built a body of music that will be sung forever, such as *Rocky Mountain High* and *Back Home Again*. From popular music, he used the themes of romance and reflection to create probably his best music. The list is almost endless but includes such popular songs as *Annie's Song* and *Sunshine*, along with more obscure but better songs, such as *The Wings That Fly Us Home* and *Singing Skies* and *Dancing Waters*.

John Denver was a pure romantic, in the best sense of the word. Although he had a keen intelligence, his heart rather than his mind ruled his actions. Love meant everything to him, and he often paid a heavy price. His heart was easily broken, yet a new love restored his hope and joy. Some of his best music resulted from either a broken heart or a newly healed one. A perfect example is *Never A Doubt:* "Oh, the magic of love, even that which is broken with love can be mended again." It was thus with John.

He always said he was one of the least prolific of songwriters, which may be true, but he didn't waste many of the songs he wrote. With a few exceptions, his music encompasses everything people need to live life to the fullest—dreams, hope, faith, trust, understanding and love. "Love is still the only dream I know," he sang in *Seasons of the Heart*. Love speaks to who John Denver was, but there is so much more. True, he made us feel, but he also made us think and he made us act upon our thoughts and dreams. Everything he sang, whether his own music or that of other composers, was offered honestly, purely, truly in a plangent voice that bared the singer's soul. This was John Denver's greatest legacy. It will never die.

RELATIONSHIPS

John asked the Dalai Lama what was the purpose of life? The Dalai Lama replied, "To be happy."

But for a man who brought much happiness to others, John experienced much unhappiness and desperate loneliness. While he sang of the purest love, John suffered heartache in relationships that offered far less than the true love he yearned for. He believed in truth and trust, but sadly discovered there were those close to him who, although putting on their best behavior with him, held diametrically opposed values to those he cultivated within himself.

John often wore a yin-yang medallion for he grasped the significance and beauty of both the male and female nature, knowing both–working together–are necessary in this life. His deep emotion sprang from the feminine within. He was unafraid to express his sensitivity. Thus, when speaking of his hope to one day take his grandchildren fishing–his hope that the environment would be secure enough to permit this-–tears formed in his eyes. And when he sang certain ballads such as *African Sunrise* or *I Want To Live* or personal songs such as *Seasons of the Heart,* he sometimes got choked up, tears welling, because the words expressed his deepest emotion.

The yin-yang medal also represented his exploration into the apparent dichotomies of life; apparent because the truth he (as many Christian mystics, Taoists, Zen Buddhists, and others) found is that which seems as opposites are actually sides of one: fire/water; air/earth; warmth/cold; male/female; life/death.

From such spiritual exploration, beautiful metaphors arise as we find in the *I'Ching (Book of Changes)* which John often read, or in Astrology, the Tarot, or the Qabalah, and in so many of John's songs. Such metaphors capture the whole of life by observing and contemplating that which our mind says are opposites, but which the heart says is part of the whole. *All This Joy, Windsong, Joseph and Joe, Zachary and Jennifer, Whalebones and Crosses, Opposite Tables, Relatively Speaking, Songs Of..., Perhaps Love,* and *Raven's Child* are some of his songs which movingly present the metaphor of apparent opposites as being one.

In seeking balance and wholeness, John understood, as he sings in *Wandering Soul,* that there is the two who desire oneness, just like "the moon whose only light is in the sun." John desired such a love more than anything in his life. As he matured, his songs reflected an understanding of such a relationship.

John possessed a strength many men lack—willingness to develop, explore and express the qualities of the feminine spirit. Understanding the necessity of embodying both the masculine and the feminine, he was unafraid to embrace both, thereby apprehending parts of the truth many men fail to realize. It became part of the spiritual power of his craft—his songs reached women and men who are introspective.

John's music drew either the deepest appreciation or complete rejection from men. It still does. Few people are ambivalent when it comes to his music. It strikes a chord within the soul—either in harmony with our spiritual values or in discord—giving us the opportunity to either listen and grow, or close ourselves—a representation of light hitting darkness. We either allow ourselves to be illuminated by it or we run away, fearful of what we will find in facing ourselves.

Countless women have told me stories of how their boyfriends or husbands will not allow John's music to be played when they're in the house and will not allow his picture to be up. These men have criticized and ridiculed their partner for mourning John's death. The pervasive male dislike of John is merely a reflection of male insecurity.

There are, however, men who look upon John as their brother—a man whom they have learned from—a man who expressed their deepest longings and emotions. These are the men who express their grief, empathize, and possess child-like wonder at the world around them. They are men like John, unafraid of the feminine within.

Being human, John knew, transcends the male or female existence into which we are born. Again, it's not about "us" or "them". It's about seeing we are one. It's about women being willing to accept the total love and devotion of a man, devotion John sings of in the magnificent *For You*. It's about women being able to appreciate a man so in love with them that the man would give his life for them, yet being able to face this world on their own without dependency on having such a man. It's about men being willing to give such love to a woman, yet never doing so in a controlling dominance. It's about human beings celebrating together the magical wonderment at two becoming one— neither more important than the other, but each working together. Such love is only possible when women embody the traits society has designated masculine (strength, courage, rationality, ability to take action) and men, characteristics regarded as feminine (compassion, empathy, sensitivity, nurturing).

John's songs cause each of us to reflect upon whether love is in our heart. If love is present, we rejoice in hearing him so beautifully express what we too feel. If love is lacking and we are receptive, we strive to make it part of us, but if our hearts are hardened, we feel resentment because we are reminded of what we are not and what we fear to be.

Why did a man who was able to realize and then communicate such truth fall victim to relationships less beautiful than the ones he sang of? Why did he yearn for such love, yet apparently never see it actualized in his life?

In *Annie's Song* or *For You*, we marvel at the wholeness of the love portrayed, and yet we know both the relationships (with his first and second wife respectively) that inspired him to write the songs proved ultimately not to be lasting love. But, the songs ring true: the dream of experiencing such a love, regardless of whether he had it in reality, brings sincerity of heart to his love songs. The love of which he sings was truly his heart's desire, though unrealized.

As John told Ray Martin, his heart longed to feel like the words he sings in *For You* or *Annie's Song*, "to really feel like that. You might feel like that for a moment, maybe the moment in which the song comes out or some night when you're singing it... But to have that the ongoing reality of your life. To wake up every morning and have someone next to you that you'd bend over right now and give your life for... just to be with that person... just to have them around."

John's remarks following his painful second divorce reflect the hurt of disillusionment and deep perplexity. He never became cynical about love despite two failed marriages, but was extremely "gun-shy" of it. For his despair, as heard in *Don't Be Kind, Seasons of the Heart, I Remember Romance* and *Different Directions,* made him weary and doubtful he would ever experience the love he longed for. Even in the loss of a relationship he had hoped would endure, he proclaimed the truth "I don't believe true love ever ends," (*Falling Out of Love*), voicing the realization that a love which ends was never truly love in the deepest spiritual sense.

John's sentiments resonate with those experiencing true spiritual love because John meant every word he wrote, and when singing such love songs, embraced not only the dream within his heart but also his experience of loving in other ways—his communion with the wilderness—as well as his love for close friends and family. As he wrote reflecting upon *Annie's Song* in the *John Denver Anthology,* "[It] is a song for all lovers and, in its deepest sense, a prayer to the love in us all." He continued, regarding *My Sweet Lady,* "I know a part of the reality occurred in my life long after I wrote the song, and I believe that some of it is yet to come true. Oh, to love like this."

The sensitivity he expressed was strength. It could only nurture any and all relationships. The weakness responsible for poor relationships (personal or business) came not from his sensitivity, but from misplaced trust and self-deception, in ignoring or compromising what was in his heart by succumbing to the temptation to see what he wanted to see rather than what was really there.

We may, as John did, fill our hearts with love and seek only to share it with another, but we must never allow ourselves to join with anyone with a different spiritual consciousness. We can, and must, be willing to engage in relationships with others for the teaching and learning experience, but it is a major mistake to accept intimately another whose heart, values, or priorities in life digress significantly from those of our own heart.

As John shared in his autobiography *Take Me Home* of his relationship with his second wife and her family, "and, being a do-gooder, I saw myself as its rescuer, its healer, just as I wanted to rescue and heal the world," but as he realized later, "there were limits to what you could do for another person." He admitted his misunderstanding of what it means to be true to oneself (instead of to one's partner), a ground rule for a wholesome relationship, when he wrote that it "said as much about me and my limitations as it did about her and where she was coming from."

Warnings signs were there, though perhaps faint in comparison to the glitter. We must heed these warnings, as John told us he neglected to do. Our intuition will tell us, others may tell us, certain circumstances and behavior will tell us—but in the whirlwind of emotional 'love' we can ignore all warnings. As John wrote after experiencing such "trials and tribulations" during the courtship, "There had already been more treachery in my life than I could bear. If it took self-deception to get through this patch, I was willing to endure it."

It requires vigilance to correctly perceive who another truly is. As Jesus told us, "Be wise as serpents, and harmless as doves."

John knew within of the beauty of what *A Course in Miracles* calls a holy relationship. A relationship (whether between friends, family, co-workers, or partners) in which the motivation of both is to joyfully share—not to take. It is a relationship in which we are not looking for anything from the other person: not security, not fun, not a family—not a thing. It's a relationship entered into by two complete persons coming together to give themselves to each other with no ulterior motives and is based first on the joining of minds and hearts. It is precisely the type of relationship every love song of John's describes; a relationship where all those other benefits—the rewards of giving and receiving in love—happen naturally, a relationship where the other's happiness is synonymous with our own.

Wanting such a relationship, as John did, is not enough. We must be strong enough to settle for nothing less. John allowed his dream of perfect love to cloud his perception—a common mistake. Settling for less can lead us to believe we have something more. Thus begins the heartache and pain.

Just as John was able to intuit and eloquently express the sorrow of those in poverty, those in war, those plagued with oppression, without actually living that life himself, so he was able to sing accurately of the joys of a holy relationship—a relationship in which two become one—though not having necessarily experienced it himself.

The essence of such a relationship is captured in his songs. From early love to mature love, from the love for children, siblings, family, close friends, to the love for a partner—John expressed truly the joy a holy relationship brings. He knew that joy within; felt such love especially for his children; and thus communicated that inner elation of true love through his songs.

As for the Dalai Lama's remark to John—despite the heartache and emotional misery he suffered, John did find happiness. Kris O'Connor describes John in 1997, "Everything was seeming to turn around. From the first of the year on, and certainly our last tour of England and Europe, he was absolutely a Prince Charming. I hadn't seen him that happy since the early days of the late 60's and early 70's. Just incredible."

As John told Dan MacDonald in a 1995 interview, "I feel I have learned a lot about myself... [I am] more capable of doing what I hope to do in the world than ever before." And though he spoke of having some real longings in his heart yet unfulfilled, he felt the most important thing he had achieved: "We spend most of our lives trying to find out who we are really... Not who you were told to be or taught to be or what someone said you ought to be. But who you are really... Therein is the real source of happiness."

And by that definition, John said, "I'm very, very happy."

In the Hearts of the Children

John loved children. There he saw true love, compassion, and unadulterated purity—the hope for humanity. Children are teachers of peace. They are precious. No matter where he was or what he was doing, a child could captivate him.

Children with their love of life, lack of guile, and ability to live completely in the moment show us the very best qualities we once had, and which we must recapture. To be child-like in our wonder for the world around us, to possess deep compassion for all living things, to want to play—is exactly how John lived. He had to deal with the concerns and difficulties of the adult world, but he never lost his capacity to experience joy as a child does. To be spontaneous, exude energy, get caught up in the intricate uniqueness of a plant or animal—he kept these things always.

With the heaviest of heart he bemoaned the plight of the child in our society today. There was a day, he would say, when children had dreamed big—seeing the whole world as open to them. The world was a place full of possibility. But, as he sadly commented, he thought that day was gone, for we, as adults, have permitted a deterioration of society, which limits their aspirations.

In his travels around the world, John saw the depths of poverty— in places such as the largest slum in the world in Bombay and in remote African villages—and in such desperate conditions of terrible malnutrition, starvation, and lack of basic hygiene, he found something beautiful: the children. The magnificent ballad, *All This Joy*, was inspired by the pure joy he saw in children who had nothing. For though they barely survived, they laughed and played, in spite of the deplorable conditions in which they lived. And though as they get older, the sparkle diminishes as they struggle just to breathe, there is hope yet. As John wrote in his "In The Hearts of Children" Windstar Vision essay in October 1991, "The children I see who are not yet teenagers do still carry the joy of childhood in their lives—even those in impoverished circumstances." These children, he said, will keep the dream alive only if those who are older do not destroy their possibilities or poison their hearts.

Although John called upon all of us to dedicate ourselves to making choices good for all, he particularly encouraged young people, who may themselves have sadly lost that dream, to seize it again. "It has to awaken in them—and stay alive in the rest of us—or we won't be able to turn things around."

It's more than instructing children with words; it's more than providing them with learning materials about preserving the Earth; it's more than sending them to nature camp. All this, though conducive to their understanding, falls short unless those young eyes see us taking action to turn the world around, see us relating to others, those with seeming differences, as our brothers and sisters. They must see love in action and be given the opportunity to share in it. Therein a world of peace, a world where humanity exists harmoniously with other life, becomes a real possibility for them to work toward—not just dry lifeless words.

Children should have no fear; neither should we. John urged us to take risks, forget what others will think of us, be ourselves. John adored children, taking delight in working with and for them. Numerous parents have handed their babies into John's arms to see the children immediately calmed and totally relaxed. He had an innate rapport with children of all ages.

The success of his children's album *All Aboard*, as well as the Muppet shows, illustrates his appeal for children and the delight he took in entertaining them. The Muppets also carried a valuable perspective for adult and child alike, as John described in an interview with Linda Hawkins: "I think the Muppets are wonderful. They're fantasy creatures and yet so human, they enable us to see ourselves objectively, from the outside, and laugh." And his Muppet appearances had long-lasting effects, as many of those originally introduced to John through them never forgot him; for many it was the beginning of an appreciation which would last for years to come. For as much as John enjoyed children, they enjoyed him. Worldwide, children still sing his songs, watch his videos, and get involved in environmental work such as tree plantings and highway clean-ups, all in John's memory.

One mother shared the simple story of how John had seen her young son fumbling through his pockets looking for change to play a video game. John came up and asked the boy what was the problem, and when he learned the child needed a quarter, John gave him four quarters. Her son immediately reached for a dollar bill and tried to give it to John, and as the mother said, "At that, John gave him a hug and told him he knew how much fun it was to play those games and this way he could play twice as many." The mother says her son now looks back and he wishes he had saved one of those quarters because it had been given to him by John.

Once, following a concert, when he was scheduled on a flight overseas and was being hurried through the arena by his staff, John spotted a group of pre-teens and began talking with them, as he often did, asking their names and hometowns, while his assistants continued to remind him he must go. According to those present, John told his men, "These children have something to say to me, and I'm going to listen to them. I will not leave until each child has had a chance to talk with me!" He then knelt down in conversation until every child had an opportunity to talk with him.

John's heart was pained when he heard of any child suffering, and often he intervened to provide what help he could. Hearing of a young boy in San Antonio, Texas, with leukemia who needed to go to Sloan-Kettering hospital for a life-saving stem cell transplant, but whose mother was single and unable to afford the trip, John sent his plane and pilot to pick them up and transport them to the hospital. He then paid for 3-months' hotel accommodation and food for the mother to stay near her son during his recovery. John telephoned the child several times and had his hospital room filled with toys. Later, John paid for their airfare back home. This example is indicative of stories nationwide where John privately and quietly helped children in need.

One caller to a radio tribute to John shared how she was at the pediatrician's office with her young son at the same time John was there with his newborn, Jesse Belle: "just to see him sitting there and holding this baby and staring at her... he really didn't even talk that much... it was more just the way he looked at her." And the only thing John actually said to this mother was, "There's nothing more precious than this life and this is why we're here."

There are many stories of how children from all over the world have responded to John's music, but the story of Jessica Smith is particularly touching, as it speaks not only to the life of one, but represents what has happened and continues to happen in children's lives because of John.

A child's wisdom surpasses that of most adults; this is the story of one such child. For Jessica was a "flower that shattered the stone." May her "innocence and trusting" teach us to be free, as John sang in *Rhymes and Reasons*.

In July 1999, Jessica Smith was returning with her family from a beautiful weekend of camping in the Rocky Mountains. And as she sat, seatbelted in her family's van, she listened joyfully to the man who was her hero—the man she admired—the man whose music had brought her newfound happiness. She was listening to her beloved John sing on her little boombox at the very moment a truck collided with their vehicle. Jessica, age 9, was killed instantly.

Jessica was no ordinary little girl. She was a child whose life had been severely traumatized by mental, emotional, and physical abuse during her first years of life. When she was adopted, at the age of four, by Lorraine and Dan Smith, she was a child whose innocence had been violated, a child with a past which could have haunted her for years to come—but with the love of her new family, and with John's music, she was healing.

One month prior to the year's anniversary of the death of this precious child, I spoke with Jessica's mother, Lorraine Smith: "About a month and half before her death, I had said I wanted *I Want To Live* by John Denver played at my funeral. [Telling young Jessica that her father might be so upset at such a time as not to do so.] 'You make sure he does honor this request.' And she said she would '*only* if you'll play John Denver at my funeral if I die before you.'"

Jessica had come a long way since they had first adopted her. "She had come through all those horrible situations and started becoming a really nice person. It was through John's music and through his ideas; it helped her get through things."

"As a four year old, she had a lot of anger inside her, but we had a lot of videos of John Denver, and *Rocky Mountain Holiday*–that was one of her favorites. She loved all the stuff done with the Muppets. This kind of turned her on to John through a child's eyes," Lorraine explained of Jessica's love for his music, but as the years went by Jessica's search for the deeper meanings in his songs became apparent.

With a loving home life and John's music, Jessica was beginning to see a new world of hope and promise around her. Her mother told of their camping trip to Colorado when Jessica was four: "We took them [Jessica and her brother] to Maroon Bells and went camping, and visited Aspen. She looked for John on every street corner... She'd say, 'Why can't we just call him and say we're in town... Can we go to lunch at his home?' She would go to every store owner and ask 'Has John been in today?' I'd tell her that's so silly, until one storeowner told Jessica that yes, John had been in just a few hours before. Jessica looked at me as though to say, 'See mom, I told you!'"

"She was so into him," and on every trip they made from their home in Texas to go camping excursions in Colorado, Jessica's focus was on seeing John.

"She was really, really different. She could be pretty and feminine, but she was also very rugged. She loved to be outside constantly. Most kids come home and they're in front of the TV immediately after school, but Jess liked to be outside. She liked to look at everything carefully. She didn't like to miss anything."

"One of the things I think John influenced her about, though she was like this anyway, was that she was so turned on to her surroundings. He's always singing and talking about every little thing and appreciate the moment, and she truly did that. That was something that really came through John as well."

Jessica knew all the words to John's songs, and stood strong against teasing from her peers because she made it no secret of her love for John's music. Says Lorraine, "She lived and breathed John Denver. While her other 9-year-old friends were off dancing to the beat of the Spice Girls, my Jessica was looking for deeper meanings in John's music. Other kids teased her about it, but he was such an inspiration to her that she remained true to John's talents even when other friends gave her a hard time about being 'uncool.' She really loved his music. It was a good example of how she didn't let the other kids influence her—the strength—the pull of his music."

"How can you not like him if he goes around preaching love all the time? I used to tell her that. When the kids teased her at school, I said think about these kids, how can they be right if they're making fun of somebody who goes around teaching love and peace all the time?"

Jessica's courage in sharing her love for John not only expressed itself in her singing and piano playing. She tried hard to find another little friend to do one of his songs with her at the school talent show, "... but nobody would. It's so pitiful." But there were times, such as at the John Denver get-together in Dallas, a year before her death, where she sang every song, never skipping a beat.

She found solace in John's music, often going to her room to work though problems. A highly intelligent child, when she was reprimanded at school for talking and knew she'd be in trouble at home for the reprimand she had received, "she would go into her room and put on one of John's songs to work through that. She automatically did that at age 8 and 9. It's amazing to me. I think his songs and words are set so you know just what to do with them."

Jessica knew, for after listening to some of her favorites such as *Love Is The Answer, Perhaps Love,* or *What Are We Making Weapons For,* she'd come out of her room in a totally fresh attitude and mood.

"He was her spiritual everything... turning her totally shattered life around... all she knew was violence," until she found the love of a nurturing family and the messages of John's songs. She constantly played, sang, and analyzed his music. Her dreams were to become a veterinarian or an environmental scientist; she was already playing in the world game by eagerly participating in highway clean-ups and other environmental projects.

The depth of her understanding of John's messages made Jessica curious about life and death in ways the majority of children are not. Death was not a taboo subject for the family. They openly discussed matters of spirituality and Jessica flourished, wondering about and comprehending things her peers had little apprehension of. The day before the truck slammed into their vehicle, Jessica had requested that a spiritual book exploring life after death be read to her as they relaxed in lawn-chairs up at their Rocky Mountain property.

Jessica, her mother said, believed that our spirit is merely inhabiting this human form, but still the thought of death "scared her big time. She didn't want to leave us. She was so excited and into living that the thought of death kind of scared her because she finally had gotten with a mom who really wanted her"—a mother who shared hiking, nature walks, and many activities with her.

"I almost think John made our bond as mother and daughter tighter. Because we had this connection—this thing we both loved to do. He kind of made a pathway for how I wanted to raise a child as far as the ethics, the love [for] everybody, and not the structured religion... John made this statement about God is in all of us, and that's very controversial as far as religious people are concerned. But that's the way I wanted to bring my kids up. Jessica was taking that from John. She was drawing her own conclusions from John's music."

Lorraine feels she and her husband have truly felt Jess with them, as John sings in Joe Henry's beautiful *The Flower That Shattered the Stone*, "Did I hear someone whisper... did something pass by?" In many different instances, Lorraine has become aware of her daughter's presence with her; "All these things are happening that are beyond strange; it doesn't fit the physical phenomena defined in science"—for it is of the spirit.

The day she died, Jessica was on her way to Rocky Mountain National Park. She wanted to see animals. In her lap was her boombox, with one of John's cassettes playing. It was the last thing she heard before she died on July 21, 1999.

Following are excerpts from the eulogy which Jessica's mother wrote
for her and which was delivered at her funeral by a spiritual advisor:

>We gather here today to join in the celebration of the life of
>Jessica Lauren Smith. She lived 9 short years, but in those 9
>years she touched so many lives and leaves the world a better
>place... She was a survivor and loved and approached life with
>such zeal... The celebrity she admired most was John Denver for
>his love of nature and humanitarian efforts. She also loved the
>deep and complicated meanings of his songs... which was pretty
>amazing for a nine-year-old. Her favorite colors—were all colors
>because she loved rainbows—she loved green the best because
>that is the color of trees and grass and she absolutely loved
>nature. She loved animals (especially cats) and they loved her
>too... Jessica loved unconditionally regardless of age, height,
>weight or looks... Jessica had many interesting ideas about love
>and what love is. The song *Perhaps Love* by John Denver was one
>of her favorites. She used to tell her mom that this song
>described her feelings towards her mom, but her mom feels that
>it describes Jessica... (*Perhaps Love* is played) ...Jessica had many
>hopes for the future. She wanted to make a difference in the
>world whether it be feeding the hungry, comforting the sick or
>preserving the environment. Her goal in life was for people to
>listen to what she had to say... Another of Jessica's favorite John
>Denver songs is *The Flower That Shattered The Stone,* written by
>Joe henry, music by John Jarvis... and sung by John Denver. She
>knew all the words by heart and wanted to learn the song on
>piano and guitar someday. To her the song meant that even
>though a person has obstacles in their life, and they may be frail
>and fragile, they can break through the barriers and blossom
>with full intensity. Well, this is exactly what she did. She was
>like a beautiful flower that had a rough start in life, but broke
>down the obstacles and was becoming an even more beautiful
>person than she was, regardless of her start in life. Please listen
>and you will visualize Jessica in every line of the song. (*The
>Flower That Shattered The Stone* is played.)

Lorraine told me she felt she had to have John's songs played at the funeral, "because I felt like if she truly could see us, I wanted her to know that I honored her wishes." One of the saddest things for Jessica's mother was that "Jessica was such a supporter of John and he needs some. It's so sad. But just the fact she liked him so much and built her life, even at the age she was at, so much around what he did and his thoughts,"—and she never was able to tell him.

Shortly after Jessica's death, Lorraine found poems in her daughter's room, poems Jess had never shared with her. This poetry reflects the heart of a child full of promise; her writings remind us of a young John, who also at such a tender age wrote his first song inspired by the Colorado River. "You can definitely see John's influence in her writings. For an 8- and 9-year-old I think they are pretty deep," Lorraine says. "I will treasure them forever."

Here are two poems Jessica wrote in 1998 at the age of 8:

The Running River

By the river there is a stone,
The river is a friend to that stone.
When the river stands still
The stone is sad about the river.
Just makes him mad.
When the water is running, the stone is happy.
When the stone is gone, the river is sad.
The feelings about the stone and the river are like mother and father.
Happy friends, happy life.
And when they are together, it's like daughter and mother
And father and son.
Life is like a gift to the river and the stone.

The Slow Forest

The city is a polluted place where everything stinks and doesn't grow,
The forest is a better and free place.
It's all shady and cool, the animals are small and free and friends.
Rocks and birds and trees are there for you and me,
Let them be free.
We all have a life and death,
Let's use the life wisely,
Let them be, let them be.

Jessica wanted to share her love of John with as many as she possibly could. She wanted to share what she could give with all the world, and she wanted to thank John and be with John and she has, and is.

A NEW AGE

66 For me, what the new age is about is breaking through that wall of
ignorance that we have lived behind to a large degree throughout
our history," John told John Esam in a 1988 interview for Australia's
New Age News.

"It's up to us to take the steps to bring it into fruition, but it's there
in the consciousness... The thought that each of us is a part of and
responsible for the quality of life on this planet, each of us is
responsible, that's new age thinking. The thought that the world used to
be you or me and now it's becoming a world of you and me—that's new
age thinking."

John's spirituality was not based on any particular precept or dogma,
rather it relied upon trust in the Spirit alone— what he needed to know
and what he should be—could be discovered in contemplative solitude.
He received inspiration and strength from the wilderness. Unlike
conventional religious doctrines, mandating certain codes of behavior
and worship, John's spiritual life was similar to that of monks and other
contemplative souls who, though they can relate to the world (which
John did exceptionally well), find inner peace on their own.

John trusted in what he perceived as the spiritual realm, no matter
what the world might say to the contrary. While the world emphasizes
caring for ourselves and our family first—he saw the human family as
one (all children were his children). While the world would have had
him conform to its fluctuating musical tastes—he endeavored to remain
true to his own. While the world engages in nationalistic pride and
separateness—he viewed himself as a global citizen. While the world
teaches us that to give something away is to lose it—John understood

giving is receiving. While the world places human beings on a hierarchy above other life forms—he understood all life is sacred. Fundamentally, the world teaches that love is impossible, but John believed love is not only possible, it is essential.

> "[He] adopts the whole connection of spiritual doctrine. He believes in miracle, in the perpetual openness of the human mind to new influx of light and power; he believes in inspiration, and in ecstasy. He wishes that the spiritual principle should be suffered to demonstrate itself to the end, in all applications to the state of man, without the admission of anything unspiritual; that is, anything positive, dogmatic, personal. Thus, the spiritual measure of inspiration is the depth of thought, and never, who said it. And so he resists all attempts to palm other rules and measures on the spirit than its own."

Although these words of Ralph Waldo Emerson could be describing John, they are from an 1842 lecture entitled "The Transcendentalist".

The philosophy of transcendentalism asserts that spiritual knowledge is more important than empirical knowledge; that there is a supernatural knowing of truth not reliant upon, or even possible to be found in, the mind's seeking; that in the heart is to be found the fundamental reality.

Although factual knowledge is used and valued, transcendentalists do not place a higher value upon it than upon their own inner guidance. Trust is put in receiving needed guidance intuitively.

Many of our greatest poets, writers, and artists have been transcendentalists, so John is in good company both intellectually and creatively. John was highly intelligent; his intellect was shown not only in his music, but in his oratory, memory, extensive knowledge, reading preferences, photography, painting and drawing, love of astronomy; keen grasp of world politics; and his writing (particularly essays). But he knew the significant difference between the spiritual and the empirical. Able to identify the constellations and planets, and even to locate and name individual stars, he could still be blown away simply by looking at the awesome beauty of a clear night sky, high in the mountains, stars twinkling brilliantly, as it "rains a fire in the sky," as he joyously sings in *Rocky Mountain High*.

"I think nature is so very important to me because it has always been my first and best friend," John explained in his *Let This Be A Voice* documentary. It's "the place where I can always find comfort, solace... where I feel, it may be funny to say, but I feel listened to and understood at a level that doesn't happen in any other aspect of life as far as I can tell."

"Funny" perhaps to the world's way of thinking, but completely understood by those who, themselves, have experienced their own communion with Spirit in such unspoiled natural solitude.

As John eloquently wrote in a 1995 article submitted to numerous media outlets in his efforts to preserve the Alaskan wilderness, "To be human is to be nourished by the wild country. To know that there is a place where the eagle flies in freedom, the grizzly walks in majesty, and the caribou runs with the wind across the open tundra, lifts the human spirit."

The spiritual communion of which John spoke is characteristic of mystics and two-fold. It is not just the feeling of being heard, it is also the experience of hearing. It is listening to the voices of the trees, the flowers, and the rocks and in so doing experiencing profoundly the presence of the divine in wilderness.

It is this experience he sings of in works such as *Tremble If You Must* where "there's life in the rocks and the seashells are listening"; in *Windsong* where the wind is "the whisper of our Mother the Earth... the hand of our Father the sky"; in *American Child* where John asks whether we hear the call of the wild to come home again to the "flowers and the trees and the rivers and the seas, and the Earth who's the Mother of all."

John loved *Boy From The Country,* the song about St. Francis of Assisi, by Murphy and Costerman, so much, he joked that he wished he'd written it. When he says of the animals speaking, "I know they do," his voice has such passion and conviction, it is clear he has experienced this himself. This entire song about St. Francis can just as appropriately be applied to John, a boy from the country who did tell us the animals could speak and that we should love the land, and who was regarded by some as less than sane because of his expressed communion with his brother the forest and his mother the Earth.

When John sings of personal rebirth in *Rocky Mountain High,* his "Talk to God and listen to the casual reply" expresses how he sought grace and found it in his true home wilderness. John's place of worship was amidst the handiwork of the Creator, not within four walls. It was a cathedral belonging to the greatest Master of all; there he found solace, love, a listening heart, and the wisdom to address his life. There he found understanding, as he never would in the world of manmade creations, or from any other human being.

Knowing "The Rockies are living, they never will die," (*Rocky Mountain Suite*) lifted his spirit in the midst of agony. He didn't just sing about it; he needed it—lived it—then sang of it. Or as he said while on a horseback ride with Ray Martin during his Australian television show, "It's here in the mountains where I'm really able to be myself and to feel what's going on. And quite often, for me, it's being by myself— getting up in the high country."

Despite his extremely busy schedule, whenever possible he retreated to the wilderness: camping at 14,000 feet in the Himalayas of Tibet; fishing in the wildness of Alaska or at Lake Taupo in New Zealand; hiking in the rainforest of Kipahulu, Hawaii; exploring Ayers Rock in Australia; observing the seals of Patagonia; enjoying the beauty of his home in the Rocky Mountains with horseback rides, skiing, astronomy, or by simply watching the golden eagles soar above. For wherever he was in the world, there was wilderness to provide what his spirit longed for—a place of complete harmonious existence—a meditative place to ease the pain.

"I will lift up mine eyes unto the hills, from whence cometh my help," (Psalms 121:1)—John did, knowing it was there he belonged.

As he despairs in *To The Wild Country,* there were times he feared he lost himself as the struggles and demands of the world were relentless. Where to go? "To the wild country," where he could again rest, renew strength, and find peace, "where I belong," he sang. It was the place where he could ski, fly, or practice his photography and put everything else aside for awhile, and "just be," as he told Jay Cowan in a 1995 interview.

John developed a rhythm of alternating time for himself and personal reflection with his extensive hours devoted to outward activities. He knew he overstepped this balance at times, and despaired when he found serenity "a long time coming to me," feeling sometimes "in fact I don't believe that I know what it means anymore," (*Eclipse*). Being away from his true home necessitated ways to keep in balance.

He had been meditating since he was eight or nine years old, and told *Playboy* interviewer Marcia Seligson in 1977, that he meditated whether he was in a car or a plane, aware of the conversations, movement, stewardesses, etc., around him, yet simultaneously going within himself in stillness and quiet.

When BBC interviewer Don Maclean asked about it, John responded, "Meditation is a very healthy thing, very good for your heart, very good for stress, and all those kind of things... you just quiet yourself down; you find that there is a place in yourself where you exist that is not the endless chatter that is going on in your mind—that is not your body—is not you physically, but is a place where you are where there is a different kind of consciousness," he continued, saying it is this awareness, which is part of every human being, that binds us together in "a very profound way."

One human family—one world—the Law of One. All John's efforts went toward the vision of making this one world. He knew there was no higher aspiration than this, and though he suffered and sometimes wondered if it was the correct choice to give so much of his life away at the expense of his own well-being, he returned to this noble dream. When he sings of its fruition in *One World*, let us not look upon it as yet another song, but as a prophecy.

He refused to be labeled as belonging to any particular political party, saying in a *Parade Magazine* interview in 1986, "I don't want to be a politician, and I don't want to pick sides." Polarization over many of his key concerns pained him, as he fervently wanted people to understand it's the good accomplished which matters—not the side proposing it.

One of the most revealing lectures John gave was one of his very first speaking engagements. Called "On Being Human," and delivered to the people of Aspen, it conveyed his enthusiasm and passion for both personal and planetary improvement. In this talk, we see his earnestness in wanting to share his spiritual basis with the world.

In it he speaks of how thrilling it is to receive letters from people telling him what his music has meant to their lives, and thus, he feels a need to share more of his thoughts, hoping people might relate to these ideas as well. Forcefully he expounds upon his understanding of the wrongfulness of separateness, saying, "I don't just believe—I know—that we're here for each other, not against each other. Yet everywhere I look in the world today, I see we take advantage of every excuse that we can to separate ourselves one from the other. Whether we're communists or capitalists; Catholic, Protestant, or Christian or Jew; whether we're businessmen or farmers; conservationist or developer; whether we're black or white; young or old; man or woman."

In this and numerous other speeches and through his music, John expressed the essence of the Law of One. As he eloquently shared in "On Being Human," it is our leaders—be they clergy, politicians, or any other societal demi-gods—who purposefully do everything in their power to make us believe in separation, as if people are different merely because of their faith, race, or political beliefs. This belief in separation gives such leaders power to herd their followers in the way that best serves their own interests. Perceived differences between ourselves and any other human being are minor compared with all we have in common, and no difference whatsoever is reason to hate, look down upon, or judge another.

Any person, or dogma which asserts that we, as part of their group, are special and set apart from others for any reason whatsoever, is in contradiction to the universal Law of One—the Law of Love.

The hope of creating one world lives in the hearts of millions, and for the first time in history, we are seeing true progress internationally in monetary systems, electronic systems of commerce and identification, and political systems. The agendas that once polarized nations are breaking down, and true hope for unity exists now more than ever.

John appreciated those of all faiths, but took exception with any which based its precepts on the exclusion or persecution of any other. As he told the *New Age News*, "I see a lot of places in the world where they are getting very hard nosed about 'this is the way,' or 'there's only one way.' I don't go along with that. I think there have been some masters in the past who have brought forth spirituality and made it real for people by their ability to articulate it." Yet isn't religion supposed to be for peace? Isn't religion supposed to draw people together, not divide?

Ironically, as John well knew, and as peace activists throughout the United States are aware, this vision of how it could be is opposed by several religious groups and organizations. In their religious zeal they fear unity, preferring instead the comfort zone of discord while falsely proclaiming their wish for peace. But their definition of "peace" holds no room for those of other faiths, for they alone are right and all others are "lost."

As John elaborated to John Esam, rejecting any religion which seeks division rather than unity, "How long has it been since they said there are many ways to Mecca? What did Jesus say? 'In my Father's house there are many mansions.' So this is coming forward."

Our spirituality, metaphysical awareness, or faith, whatever form it takes, is linked either to our oneness with all, or our belief in differences. No one believing in separateness is for peace, regardless of how hard they might argue. In the midst of their vocal protestations to the contrary, their hypocrisy becomes all the more apparent.

John gave wholehearted support to the United Nations (even donating the profits from his song *Rhymes and Reasons* to UNICEF to battle starvation), seeing the UN as the only political entity which was trying to bring unity, rather than diversion. He deplored the fact his nation, the United States, spent so much on weaponry and so little in comparison on helping developing nations. He was, he said on a 1990 *Geraldo* show, "embarrassed that of the 18 wealthy nations in the world which are working on ending world hunger, in regard to the percentage of gross national product providing help to developing nations, we [the US] rank like 15 or 16."

One might think in the ten years which have elapsed, the U.S. and the other wealthiest countries might finally have placed social/humanitarian priorities above the military build-up, but a report issued in June 2000 by UNICEF, shows that one in six children in the world's richest nations live in poverty, with the United States and Britain being two of the worst offenders (in relation to the wealth of the nation versus percentage of children in poverty). While the 'civilized' nations of the world adhere to the UN's Declaration of Human Rights rejecting capital punishment, the U.S. continues in the state-sanctioned killing of its citizens. While other nations such as Norway and Sweden make it a national priority to stop children living in poverty, the U.S. lags behind. While other systems ensure the basic human needs of food, shelter, and medical care, our capitalistic society thrives as some of its citizens suffer.

"It's about time to turn the world around," John sang in *It's About Time*. As people worldwide strive to make peace the reality, it is time for wealthy nations to rise and implement new policies, providing basics: shelter, food, medical care, electricity, and transportation to the poorest of their citizens. Continuing to "feed the war machine" as John lamented in *Let Us Begin*, occurs at the expense of our people. Corporate indifference, seeking profit above the people's interest, leads to poverty and environmental destruction. Greed maintains the status quo; some things do not belong in the hands of the market place.

This is the message John wanted earnestly to communicate and until it becomes what he called "the popular will," it shall never become the "political will." It requires cooperation among religious and non-religious groups—Christians, Jews, Muslims, Hindus, Buddhists, Humanists, and every other faith, and every governmental entity.

John encouraged grassroots activism. To speak out; to organize community projects for the human beings hurting right where we live; to make changes in our daily lives and in our consumption habits; to feed the hungry right in our own cities; to visit the old; to forego judgement and be someone who helps and assists those in jails and prisons; to spend time with the mentally impaired; to do our very own highway clean-up—and not wait for it to be organized.

To work for peace means making ourselves vulnerable to the spears and arrows of the opposition. It means sacrifice. It means giving up some of what we have—be it time, money, or possessions. It means simply opening our eyes, because if we do we'll see someone needing help we can give. It means doing something regardless of whether anyone else around us is doing it. It is, as he sings in *World Game*, "choosing less and doing so much more."

For as John states in *It's A Possibility*, "Though the heart is just a lover, it's never afraid to fight." We are fighting for more than survival, more than peace (more than merely the absence of killing)–we are fighting to make sure "all injustice will someday cease."

Spiritual advancement, John believed, is an integral part of realizing Heaven on Earth.

Instrumental to upholding the Law of One is willingness to recognize that the terrible injustices and evil committed in this world are our responsibility. This is the meaning behind, "The source of our sorrow and shame... we are one," in the powerful *Raven's Child*. One whose greed makes decisions; one who murders; one who steals; one who betrays; one who lies; one who has committed the worst crimes imaginable; we are no different, in essence. We have the ability to do the very same or similar dark deeds. Only by acknowledging this can we love those who do such deeds, thereby using our heart and mind (what John called "this incredible tool") to be part of the good in the world.

As Robert Fulghum wrote in his wisdom-packed book, *It Was On Fire When I lay Down On It*, "The line between good and evil, hope and despair, does not divide the world between 'us' and 'them.' It runs down the middle of every one of us. I do not want to talk about what you understand about this world. I want to know what you will *do* about it. I do not know want to know what you *hope*. I want to know what you will *work for*. I do not want your sympathy for the needs of humanity. I want your muscle."

John also looked toward mental, physical, and philosophical and religious/spiritual practices for their heightening effect upon his life, finding real value in a variety of areas: diet, breathing exercises, acupuncture, pyramids, accupressure, yoga, reiki, Rolfing, chiropractic, astrology, physical fitness, and posture exercises. He studied Buddhism (Zen), the *Tao Te Ching* and *I'Ching*. Whether passing the peace pipe around in a sacred Native American ceremony or exploring his earliest recollections in spiritual regression with his shaman, John was open to understanding of truth wherever he might find it.

For many years John worked with astrology and also threw the *I'Ching* practically every day (and often quoted from its text). The

I'Ching is an ancient means of divination based upon synchronicity (meaningful coincidence) in which the answers to questions are divined by throwing sticks or coins and a chart of hexagrams is consulted, denoting a particular part of the text to be read.

But such practices were merely tools he used to help attain the spiritual, emotional, and physical wellness he desired; they were not the way. They are not the means to understanding in themselves.

True enlightenment begins when we surrender and open ourselves by simply proclaiming we are open, ready, and willing to serve. John did this at an early age; he became what the Tao would refer to as an "evolved individual."

A favorite book of John's, *The TAO—The Watercourse Way,* written by Alan Watts in collaboration with John's friend, Al Chung-liang Huang, explores Contemplative Taoism—what Buddhists call the *Way of Wisdom.* At the root of Taoism lies a way of living effortlessly with nothing left undone. *The TAO* shows us how to approach every single event, or every action we take, without stress, despite the hard work that may be required. The 'watercourse' speaks to the stream of life. We are in the Tao whether we realize it or not—for the Tao is the way of life.

The Tao, being the ultimate reality, exists and we are part of it. Choosing to learn its way brings contentment and freedom from much of the stresses we currently undergo. Choosing to deny it means more strife in our lives as we meander full of confusion, trying desperately to understand the meaningless. Illusory precepts will always fail us. The Tao never fails; it simply is, and studying it and applying its principles in our lives lessens suffering: for nothing causes more pain than the attempt to understand our lives or the lives of those around us based on illusionary concepts. Reading *The TAO* brings John's songs to mind. "Like a fish in the water... like a bird in the air" (*Sweet Surrender)* is the way—the Tao. "All this joy... all this sorrow... All this promise... all this pain" (*All This Joy)* is the way—the Tao.

The TAO is a textbook of enlightenment, lifting our perceptions to the simple truths: All are one; trust; fight when necessary and with regret; that which seems unpredictable and capricious is actually a result of our own being and doing; resist not the experiences of life—be they 'good' or 'bad'; do not egoistically seek to know truth by intentionally reading, meditating, or performing artificial 'spiritual' practices in hopes of improving understanding, rather follow your inner intuition and the way will be revealed.

The Tao is about trusting in ourselves, holding out no matter what for the truth within us. The Tibetan word for wisdom is *yeshe*, meaning primordial intelligence. It is what we were born with—complete truth—and it's what we must place above all other matters in life as John did.

As a boy, John felt pain seeing the mistreatment and the cruelty perpetrated by some children upon others. In high school he felt pain seeing a young girl continually being ridiculed because of her appearance and mental disability. At college he felt pain seeing his peers laughing at a young man who stuttered. He was so attuned to truth—to the Law of One—that when these precious people were taunted, it was as if he himself was being taunted.

Empathy—identification with another entity to such a degree its deprivation is felt as our own—is the highest form of spirituality. . It is what Buddhism calls a mark of an "enlightened being." John exhibited empathy for all human beings, as well as every thing—inanimate and animate—on Earth. Because his peers lacked such compassion, John felt different when he was young

In a series of lectures given in Boulder, Colorado in 1970 and 1971, Chögyam Trungpa, once the supreme abbot of the Surmang monasteries in eastern Tibet before he was forced to leave his country by the Chinese Communist takeover in 1959, differentiated between conventional compassion and the true compassion of someone like John.

The Buddhist teacher described two types of false love many of us exhibit: "Either we are being fed by someone or we are feeding others." In other words, one type is the need to belong to another, committing ourselves to some person—parent, teacher, or partner—or to a religion or other organization, and clinging desperately so that we feel accepted and cared for. The other type is the need to relate to another person or organization as if we could fulfill all their needs, making them our child, so to speak, so this person or group is dependent upon us. Neither of these pervasive behaviors is love, for both stem from an egotistical 'compassion' which seeks either to rely completely upon another so that we feel loved, or to make another dependent upon us so that we may have power over them. This is the common 'compassion' millions of people engage in, simply to make themselves feel good about who they are—thus in service to their own egos rather than in service to others.

Although it may benefit others, this false love is given from self-serving motives: the elimination of guilt, the gratification of the ego (from being praised by others), and for profit, emotional comfort, or power. Examples of such adulterated love are: corporations publicizing their "generosity" by giving miniscule percentages of their profit to a charity; those who do "good works" to bask in the public recognition they receive; family members or friends desiring approval from others or wanting control over them. Anyone who seeks to gain in a relationship, regardless of the form it takes, is exhibiting false love.

"Who has the right to see how far it can bend?" John asks in *World Game,* for love requires nothing in exchange.

Love relates openly, giving when it identifies a need and receiving when it has a need. As John explained, if we feel there's nothing out there that's loving and comforting for us, it is because there is nothing in us—in our own heart—which are those things to others.

As Chögyam Trungpa eloquently said, "Just be what you are. You do not reduce yourself to the level of an infant nor do you demand that another person leap into your lap. You simply be what you are in the world, in life... Then you can communicate directly and accurately, not indulging in any kind of nonsense, any kind of emotional or philosophical or psychological interpretation... a balanced way of openness and communication which automatically allows tremendous space, room for creative development, space in which to dance and exchange," (from the lectures of Trungpa in *Cutting Through Spiritual Materialism*).

Love is open giving—as Trungpa continued; it's a real openness on a huge scale, "a revolutionary large and open scale, a universal scale." It's the scale and openness John taught us when he sang of "choosing less and doing so much more" (*World Game*).

John spoke of a reality beyond the physical. Throughout his life he experienced instances of clairvoyance, as well as recognizing so much of his music was coming to him from a greater power. He embraced the supernatural or metaphysical.

Clairvoyance was a power he knew he had and sought to develop. There were several incidents of it; the most well-known is when John, ten days prior to adopting his son Zachary, had a dream in which into his arms was placed a dark-skinned baby boy, with an overbite, who grabbed John's thumb and smiled. John and his wife had no idea of the sex, race, or physical appearance of the child they were to receive. True to the dream, ten days later, the couple were handed young Zachary—and the child was identical to the baby in his dream—and, yes, their new son immediately grabbed John's thumb and smiled. There, as John has said, a dream met reality. This is but one example of many such experiences John alluded to over the years.

In a time of numerous unorthodox approaches to human spirituality, John was often asked his feelings on what many people term new age thinking. He spoke specifically upon this topic to the Mile Hi Church of Religious Science in Denver in 1988, imploring people not to fear new age thinking.

He acknowledged that crystals and pyramids and channeling are all manifestations of the same spiritual search—a quest for understanding. (He also shared his own love of crystals and how in a temple he had visited recently, a magnificent crystal had caused his hands to vibrate.) He then spoke of a recent meeting with Gorbachev in which Gorbachev told him there was a new reality in the world—a reality which can't survive with a focus on self interest—a reality, Gorbachev said, requiring consideration of others' needs. "That's," said John, "new age thinking, in my opinion."

John then told of his trip to a remote village in Africa's Burkina Faso—an area with an extremely high infant mortality rate—where he asked the chief how drought was affecting the people. To John's surprise, the chief described the drought as a great tool because it had taught his people to work together because of their need to conserve water. Prior to the drought, the chief explained, the people only took care of themselves and now they cared for each other. Again, John said, "New age thinking."

The lecture at Mile Hi Church not only gave insight into John's approach to new age matters, but also revealed his deep respect for those who attended this church. He even remarked that his worshipping with the congregation felt so comfortable to him that it was like "coming home to a place I've never been before." (*Rocky Mountain High*)

A Religious Science church such as Mile Hi found him in the company of an entire congregation of people with whom—to his amazement—he shared many teachings and beliefs: that individuals control the course of their lives, creating their experiences with the power of their thoughts; that oneness, that supreme creative Power of the universe, the source of all substance, is present throughout the universe and in each of us; that God is love, and love is the divinity which is in all and blesses all.

Mile Hi was a church whose vision was "a world in which we live as One Human Family, in spiritual partnership for the good of all life," a church whose stated purpose was "to serve as a spiritual beacon, lighting the way for the discovery and expression of every person's inherent divinity and infinite possibilities," a church where, to his expressed surprise, he felt at home.

John quoted from the Mile Hi mission statement, "The Science of Mind is a philosophy, a faith, and a way of life dedicated to awakening the conscious experience and expression of every person's Divine nature." It was, as John said, a church whose mission, whose people and their purpose, originated from the same place he wished to speak to them from in his own heart.

Within this speech, John expressed his assessment of the spiritual state of the planet: "It's like the Renaissance so many hundreds of years ago... Perhaps it's the age of Aquarius that we talked about in the late 60's and early 70's..."

"Or," he continued, "Perhaps it really is the kingdom of Heaven on Earth coming into a kind of manifestation and reality that's never been here before..."

"A new age." Let it be.

LOVE IN ACTION

"I shall become enlightened for the sake of all living things."–a Buddhist vow.

John's musical achievement is unprecedented: breaking record sales worldwide–a list of musical accomplishments which numbers many pages. People around the world treasured his music. But this is not the place to elaborate on his musical achievements. The benefits of his success in music, movies, and television specials gave him the ability to devote himself to the things he believed. Though his dedication to his career meant giving much up personally, it provided the means to better the world and inspired others to do the same.

As John's friend, Tom Poberezny, President of the Experimental Aircraft Association, told me, "When John supported something, he did it because he wanted to. Not because it was politically correct or whatever. John was one of the most articulate persons I've ever met; sincere and dedicated to what he believed in. Because he was a talented person, he could use that to gain a platform for his messages, and he wasn't afraid to do that."

Chuck Woolery, Issues Advocacy Director of the World Federalist Association, viewed John similarly: "John's political positions and writings on world hunger really inspired me to get involved 22 years ago. His willingness to use his celebrity status in political issues, at that point in time, made him one of the first who did that. Before that, I had an aversion to working in politics. [But seeing John's service on the Presidential Commission on World and Domestic Hunger and hearing its findings changed that.] He blew away the myths I had about hunger and really documented how it was the political will that was missing. So, from that point on I started to get involved in politics." Woolery then became an activist in the Hunger Project, as well as being with the World Federalist Association and serving on the Action Board of the American Public Health Association.

Few individuals' lives reflect such incredible passion. It is important in honoring John's memory to take note of his environmental and humanitarian work, as it is this which reflects accurately his spirituality.

The following is a partial list of activities in which John was involved. It is only a fraction of his altruistic works, as much of his giving was done privately. It includes, too, some of his achievements, a few of the awards bestowed upon him, and some of the many organizations with which he was involved.

These are some of the awards he received:

• **Albert Schweitzer Music Award:** bestowed upon John, the first non-classical artist to ever receive this prestigious honor for "a life's work dedicated to music and devoted to humanity." John's activism exemplified Schweitzer's definition of Reverence for Life, which "contains all the components of ethics: love, kindliness, sympathy, empathy, peacefulness, power to forgive."

• **Friends of the Universe Award:** from the CLEAN (Citizens Looking Ecologically Ahead Now) Foundation in Canada.

• **Freedom of Flight Award:** the Experimental Aircraft Association's highest honor presented to John in recognition of his "contributions to aviation and our society."

• **International Center for Tropical Ecology World Ecology Medal:** "He gave inspiration to everyone," says ICTE Director Dr. Bette Loiselle of John, who was the first recipient of the international award for commitment to the environment. The ICTE now awards a scholarship annually in John's memory to help students conduct field research in tropical biodiversity as they pursue their graduate education.

- **U.S. Jaycees' Ten Outstanding Men of America Award:** Winners of this award exemplify the principles of the Jaycees, whose creed includes, "Earth's great treasure lies in the human personality," and "Service to humanity is the best work of life."

- **NASA Medal for Public Service:** for helping "increase awareness of space exploration by the people of the world." John flew and landed the space shuttle simulator in preparation for possibly becoming the first civilian in space, passed NASA's physical/mental exam, was Master of Ceremonies at the Goddard Dinner, and attended the launch of *Apollo/Soyuz*, and other launches and landings.

- **National Wildlife Federation Conservation Achievement Award:** It was with NWF President, Jay Hair, that John scouted the environmental destruction and recovery attempts at Prince William Sound, following the Exxon *Valdez* disaster, inspiring *Raven's Child*.

- **World Without Hunger Award** given by President Ronald Reagan.

- **Whale Protection Fund Service Award.**

The following awards were received for John's documentary *Rocky Mountain Reunion* (a film devoted to animals threatened with extinction and efforts to ensure their survival by finding homes for rare creatures such as the golden eagle, the trumpeter swan, the wolverine, and the grizzly bear):

- **Western Heritage Center's National Cowboy Hall of Fame Award for Most Outstanding Factual Documentary;**

- **Freedom Foundation at Valley Forge George Washington Award for Best Documentary of the Year;**

- **CINE Golden Eagle Award for Excellence in Representing the United States Internationally in Film Abroad;**

- **American Film Festival New York City Blue Ribbon Award–Best Educational Film;**

- Denver International Film Festival Award—Outstanding Achievement in Film Making;

- Best Outdoor Travel/Recreational Film—Michigan Outdoor Writers Association.

For *The Higher We Fly* film:

- Earl D. Osborn Award—Outstanding Excellence on Subject of Aviation from Aviation/Space Writers' Association.

As a founder, a director, an advisor, or simply as a member, John donated time and money or otherwise placed his support behind the following organizations and causes:

- **Aspen Camp School For The Deaf:** "His love for children and his special caring for deaf and hard-of-hearing youth was ever-present throughout his involvement with the Deaf Camp," said Executive Director B.J. Brubaker Blocker; "In our formative years, he helped by performing at benefit concerts for the Camp. His last concert here in Roaring Fork Valley was a spectacular performance in Snowmass Village in 1997 celebrating the Camp's Twenty-fifth Anniversary." The entire Camp remembers John "for his many contributions to the children."

- **Aspen Valley Hospital:** "I think the entire hospital community is grateful to John Denver for his generous assistance over the years in providing needed funds for capital improvements, especially [for] the labor and delivery area, as well as [for his] participation in the purchase of new state of the art diagnostic equipment," said Kris Marsh, Executive Director. of the Aspen Valley Medical Foundation. John's gifts throughout 1975–1977 were approximately $126,000 with an additional $15,000 donation toward purchase of a CAT scan in 1989. Marsh says the high quality care they provide is "way above what a normal small town would be able to provide" due to gifts such as John's.

- **Challenger Center:** John donated royalties from his tribute song *Flying For Me* (in memory of the 51-L crew: Gregory B. Jarvis, Christa

McAuliffe, Ronald E. McNair, Ellsion S. Onizuka, Judy A. Resnik, Dick Scobee, Michael J. Smith) to the *Challenger* families.

• **Cousteau Society:** John became close friends with Jacques Cousteau, bringing needed publicity to Cousteau's environmental message and donating proceeds from *Calypso* to further the work.

• **Experimental Aircraft Association:** Actively involved in teaching young people the joys of aviation. John attended annual fly-ins, made educational films, and donated money for the building of facilities for the Young Eagles; he was an active member of the EAA for over 20 years. Says EAA President, Poberezny, of John, "...a wonderful spokesman."

• **The Hunger Project:** One of the five founders of the Project, John took Keith Bloom's powerful documentary to U.S. legislators as he lobbied to bring hunger to the forefront of the government's agenda. He appeared on television shows, gave lectures nationwide, and diligently committed himself to the Project. He traveled to famine-ridden villages in Africa and to the slums of Bombay. *I Want To Live* was written as a voice for the starving children, and *African Sunrise* was written from John's experience of awaking in an African village to a strange sound mixed with the crowing of the roosters—and realizing the unusual sound was the last cries of babies dying from starvation. John gave a benefit concert for the Project after its global board meeting, and sang for Hunger Project participants in India, Europe, the U.S. and Africa.

• **National Arbor Day Foundation:** John wrote the music and lyrics for *Plant A Tree* and recorded 19 Public Service Announcements.

• **National Space Institute:** John was the catalyst for the citizens in space program; he spoke before the Senate subcommittee regarding the intrinsic value of space exploration. An original member of the National Space Institute's governing board since 1976, he remained involved when the NSI merged with the L-5 society, forming the National Space Society. In a press release following John's death, Chairman of the NSS Board of Governors, Hugh Downs, said, "From the beginning, John knew what he wanted to do... We will miss his vision, his talent, his perseverance and his unique ability, through his words and music, to help others understand the fragility and beauty of this planet we call home."

• **Nuclear Safeguards:** John gave benefit concerts, donated money and campaigned.

• **Preservation of Alaskan Wilderness:** From the 1970's onward, John diligently fought to conserve millions of acres of the wilderness lands of Alaska; he fought against opening the coastal plain to oil exploration, which he believed endangered the delicate ecosystem, and for the preservation of the Arctic National Wildlife Refuge, his help having been requested by the Northern Alaska Environmental Center. John was invited to attend President Carter's Oval Office signing of the Alaska National Interest Lands Conservation Act into law.

• **Presidential Commission on World and Domestic Hunger:** Because of his involvement in the Hunger Project, John was appointed to this fact-finding task force by President Jimmy Carter.

• **United Nations/UNICEF** (United Nations Children's Fund): John hosted programs for UNICEF and donated the proceeds from *Rhymes and Reasons* to the fund. He appeared in the United Nation's Association of Minnesota's film *Man's Next Giant Leap,* which was shown at schools and service clubs to educate viewers that the family of man's hope for a permanent peace is through the United Nations.

• **Wildlife Conservation Society:** He performed *The Wildlife Concert* (A&E/Sony), made recordings for the WCS, and served on its Board of Advisors. The President of the WCS, Dr. William Conway said of John to me, "You couldn't help but be moved by the man."

• **World Federalist Association:** John served on the Board of Advisors of this organization whose vision is for "a democratic world federation limited to achieving positive global goals that nations cannot accomplish alone."

• **Wyoming protection:** He did benefits for West Star Productions and the Snake River Institute, and a benefit for the Murie Center in Jackson

Hole of Grand Teton National Park where his friend, the remarkable environmentalist, Mardy Murie, lived.

(John also supported: Alaska Coalition, Aspen Center of Environmental Studies, Aspen Global Change Institute, Center for Attitudinal Healing, Environmental Action, Environmental Defense Fund, EST, First Earth Run, Friends for all Children, Friends for Animals, Friends of the Earth, Human/Dolphin Foundation, Kushi Foundation, Music Associates of Aspen, New Earth Exposition, Plant-It 2000, Native American Assistance, Save The Children, Sierra Club, Special Olympics, U.S. Skiers Education Fund, Wilderness Society, Windstar Foundation, World Wildlife Fund, Worldwide Nature Fund.)

Other activities:

John took part in what some regarded as politically subversive music, homecoming concerts, rallies, and student demonstrations to end the Vietnam War (his Chad Mitchell Trio days), as well as in support of the civil rights movement of the United States.

His commitment to further East/West understanding found him making trips to the Soviet Union. His visit to the cemetery of Piskaryovka where 470,000 are buried who died during the nine-hundred-day siege of Leningrad, inspired the creation of *Let Us Begin*. He performed throughout the Soviet Union in 1984–1986 by invitation of Soviet Union of Composers, the first Western artist to do so since the cultural exchanges between the two nations had been suspended. He was a catalyst for the signing of the cultural agreement between the U.S. and the USSR in 1985. He returned in 1987 for a benefit concert in the Ukraine, by invitation of Dr. Armand Hammer, for victims of the Chernobyl accident. John was also, in 199w, the first westerner to do a multi-city tour of mainland China, as well as the first westerner, after the Vietnam War ended, to perform in Hanoi and in Ho Chi Min City.

He also participated in benefit concerts, ski tournaments, and golf tournaments throughout his career with proceeds going to many environmental and humanitarian causes. He gave personal assistance, such as truckloads of toys delivered anonymously to Native American reservations, and provided transportation and money for children's medical care.

He gave numerous lectures and speeches to university and governmental groups and to churches and metaphysical gatherings throughout the world regarding environmentalism and humanitarian work through development of the Spirit.

THE CIRCLE OF LIFE

There is no better way to honor John than to approach every situation in life with these questions: How can I help? What is the most loving action I can take?

An often quoted song of his, *On The Wings of a Dream,* says although the singer is silent, we still have the truth of his song. John was a mentor. He did not seek self-glorification; he sought only to share with others what he himself had learned.

In his book *Mentoring*, Edward C. Sellner writes: "All mentoring, especially spiritual mentoring, is a form of empowerment that helps others discern their vocations, acknowledge their gifts and begin to give shape to their dreams."

We must not be reliant upon our religion, our country, or even our mentors to create the world we want. What matters is that the divine spark, goodness, light—however we conceive of it—lives through each of us. We are the instruments of peace. If humankind is to find solutions to the monumental problems we have created, we must look to ourselves to create by conscious choice the solutions.

"Conscious choice" was one of John's favorite phrases. Perhaps we can look to the words of the seventh century poet Shantideva and proclaim them as our commitment, for they are clearly reflective of an inner vow John took early in life:

> For I have taken upon myself, by my own will, the whole of the pain of all living things. Thus I dare try every abode of pain, in... every part of the universe, for I must not defraud the world of the root of good. I resolve to dwell in each state of misfortune

through countless ages... for the salvation of all beings... for it is better that I alone suffer than that all beings sink to the worlds of misfortune... I venture to stand surety for all beings, speaking the truth, trustworthy, not breaking my word. I shall not forsake them... I must so bring to fruition the root of goodness that all beings find the utmost joy, unheard of joy, the joy of omniscience. I must be their charioteer, I must be their leader, I must be their torchbearer, I must be their guide to safety... I must not wait for the help of another, nor must I lose my resolution and leave my tasks to another. I must not turn back in my efforts to save all beings nor cease to use my merit for the destruction of all pain. And I must not be satisfied with small successes.

(Selection of the Shantideva from the anthology *World of the Buddha: A Reader* edited by Lucien Stryk)

If all who appreciate John live the love he sang of and demonstrated, we can create heaven on earth. It means being willing to embrace all which life brings us—the pain, the sorrow, and the joy. There's a Buddhist saying of the Bodhisattva, an enlightened one who chooses to remain in this world: "All life is sorrowful." It is impossible to be here and not suffer. But, some choose it as the means to help others see who they truly are and what they are capable of.

Native Americans speak of the Medicine Wheel, or the Circle of Life. The Circle of Life is all change—birth, learning, living, and dying. It is the cycle of all which exists, showing every life is dependent on all others. Each death, too, serves a greater purpose for those whose eyes can see. Often the death of a great teacher brings about an even greater devotion to the teaching.

John was given his Native American name, "Sees the Eagle," from the Fort Belknap Assiniboine and Gros Ventre (White Clay People) of Montana as a special gift. The eagle, representative of the freedom John desired for everyone, himself included, was highly significant to him. John exemplified the attributes of the eagle: its strength—he was ready to fight for Earth's survival; its nurturing of its young—he cared for the whole of humanity; its eye for detail—he saw clear and far; its freedom of flight—he soared above the cares of the world. The eagle spoke to John in visions, dreams, and in the physical world.

Native American elders use the Circle, or Medicine Wheel, as a mirror. Elders have said, "The Universe is the Mirror of the People, and each person is a Mirror to every other person," (*Seven Arrows* by Hyemeyohsts Storm).

Anything serving to remind us of the cycle of life, any idea, object, ritual, or person, can be a Medicine Wheel. For many it is John. Finding our place "in this mirror sea" (*Zachary & Jennifer)* means seeking to perceive the harmony we share with all by giving to all. John has provided us with the gateway, we have taken steps on the way, but to fulfill our purpose, we must do as he did: allow love to govern every action and celebrate life.

I am reminded of a beautiful quotation from the writer Edith Wharton, "There are two ways of spreading light: to be the candle or the mirror that reflects it."

If you see John as a candle for your life, reflect what you have learned. Don't be content to merely speak well of him, play his music, and identify yourself as someone who appreciates him. No. Doing only those things is missing the point. Don't be content with an annual gathering to honor him. You will do all that and far more when you endeavor to put the love he exemplified into action in your life now.

In so doing, you will become a candle for others—another point of the medicine wheel.

It will take far more than simply expressing your hopes and dreams for a better world. A cry for peace shows only the desire, but until that desire manifests itself into real-time action, peace will remain only a dream.

Love is due every human being we meet. Not one is unworthy of love. Love is due every sentient creature—from an ant crawling on the sidewalk to a great whale. Love is due even that which seems inanimate—the rocks, trees, all of Earth, right down to "a blade of grass," John said.

Discernment is the listening that precedes action. More than deciding the action to take—it is attunement of our hearts so that every note of clarity is felt within us—within our emotions, our mind, and our will.

Spiritual discernment will be enhanced by meditation upon his music. John's music, as he commented, did not belong to him. It belongs to all of us. His music illumines the path to freedom from material, intellectual, and emotional bondage, so we can play in the world game effectively.

The cumulative wisdom John found through his lifelong search for truth is there to help unite mind with soul so we may take action. For example, you may be told to immediately go and take an action (perhaps benefiting someone or something) you never dreamed of taking. Your worldly mind will immediately cast doubt upon your plans, throwing question after question at you—all the good reasons not to do what has just come to you. At such times, heed John's advice: "Your spirit, your faith must be strong" (*What One Man Can Do*).

Love is powerful—but it only works when we work it.

It is this hurdle John wanted more than anything for us to surpass. How many times was he asked, "What can I do, the problems are so big?"

Yes, the problems are great John said. Change doesn't happen quickly when it's the spiritual consciousness, or lack thereof, we are up against. Change happens as each individual says, "Here I am. How can I help?" It is truly "now or never, do or die," as he sang in *High, Wide and Handsome*.

Though accepting the mission is stressful, the truth is: "Without a battle there is no victory; without a challenge there is no life." (*Wild Rivers and Mountain Trails* by Don Ian Smith).

Prior to John's death, I went through times of confusion. As he sings in *Singing Skies and Dancing Waters*, "Somehow in reason, I'd lost sight of seasons," and my heart would ask "Are you still with me?" The clarity and resounding "Yes" came only after his passing.

Perhaps it was thinking I should have had the answers to all my questions, or perhaps it was thinking John should have had them. The realization that he, too, had weaknesses as we all do, strengthens my faith, though it took time to fully comprehend this. But "in the heart, and in the spirit, and in the truth" *Singing Skies and Dancing Waters* there is full understanding.

Healing has brought the realization life is both joy and sorrow—promise and pain—for "such is spirit, such is love." (*All This Joy*). Healing has brought the deepest knowledge that in the "darkest of nights, I was never ever alone" (*Love is the Master*). It is time for all who have experienced this to make his dream reality, for all are called to be miracle workers.

John's transition reminds me of what Chung-tzu wrote on the death of Lao-tzu: "The Master came because it was time. He left because he followed the natural flow... The wood is consumed but the fire burns on, and we do not know when it will come to an end."

It is healing time.

"That means being willing to let go, to honor death in order to receive new life," John wrote in his essay "Springtime—New Beginnings" in the *Plant-A-Tree Tour Book*. Here he tells us how we as humans somehow "get caught up in the insecurity of the unknown. We forget that change is actually essential to continuing life."

John cited nature as representative of this truth: a snake shedding its skin, a lobster its shell, the transformation of a pupa to butterfly, the seasons. Change. "As humans, we need to be courageous and surrender to that reality," he wrote.

If we have the courage to honor John's life, his death—his change—will bring renewal, and that renewal, as John said, will require us "to go inside ourselves to hear our most authentic voice." There we will learn how to be free of the past. The process of renewal within ourselves will not happen and we will not reach our potential unless we recognize what John believed, that new beginnings and growth do not occur until after a "dramatic" change—sometimes a "real death."

His death has meant transformation, a time for the rebirth and healing he sang of in *Let The Mountains Talk*—a time for remembering who we are, "the seed within a bright and shining star," by letting go of all fear and embracing love as the "reason... the why... the answer... the way," as he told us in *Wandering Soul*.

In the 1995 Choices symposium John said the song he felt best expressed his greatest longing and deepest commitment was

Amazon/Let This Be A Voice, and his hope was that its message, "Let this be a voice for the forests... the oceans... the children [would] to some degree express a longing that lives in each of you and a commitment... that *your* voice—the collective voice we have—can be a voice for all of our dreams."

I believe John would have us know that "[I am in] a haven for my spirit, the homeland of my dreams... My heart flies through the wilderness and on an eagle's wings... to the place where Earth and heaven meet and [I am] forever in my song... I carry you along." (*Durango Mountain Cabellero*)

"The country knows not yet, or in the least part, how great a son it has lost... He had in a short life exhausted the capabilities of this world... Wherever there is knowledge, wherever there is virtue, wherever there is beauty, he will find a home." (words of Emerson at the passing of Thoreau)

John is home.

THE MEMORIALS

After writing the international tribute for John, there were times when deep emotion overcame me and I needed to write to clarify my feelings as I resolved the grief I felt. From those occurences came the memorials for John–each reflective of my path of healing the pain and renewal of my commitment to "play in the world game" (*World Game*) despite John's loss.

The memorials were written approximately six months apart... I share them here in the order they were written.

John: "A Friend to All the Universe– Everything that I Would Like to Be"

I was four years old, and on a sunny afternoon in 1971, I fell in love. And, it was a love which will last my lifetime.

I still vividly recall it: pedaling down an earthen country road on my red tricycle; the warmth of the sun upon my back; my father walking beside me. I was having the time of my life.

Then, something magical happened– a tune from the transistor radio my father was carrying suddenly captivated me and I knew something very special was occurring.

The song that delightful day was John Denver's *Take Me Home Country Roads*. It was then and there that my love and appreciation for him and his beautiful music began.

His music has spoken to my heart throughout my life. Now, my mind is filled with a welter of emotions as I recall just how significant and meaningful John has been and always will be to me.

Throughout the 70's, I spent my childhood declaring, "The only man I ever want to marry is John Denver." It was the innocent appreciation that a little girl expressed for his wonderful music, his appearances with the Muppets and in the film *Oh, God.* But, no. It was actually something more.

As I matured into my teens in the 80's, I found that John's music was crucial to who I was becoming. I didn't care whether he was considered popular. He was essential to helping me grow spiritually, as I discovered the things which would remain important to me to this day.

It was John who nurtured my concern for the environment, motivating me to get involved in protecting our magnificent wildlife and wilderness. It was his deep commitment as evidenced in his music and activities which made my appreciation deepen. It was his willingness to get involved in worldwide efforts for peace that helped me become the person I am now: someone who must "play in the World Game," someone who deeply desires to "make it better than it's ever been before." It was that song, *World Game*, which became a driving force within me, for I also wanted to help make a difference... somehow.

It was also John who gave me and my father strength to continue to pursue our dream of moving to the Rocky Mountains. For so many years that dream lived within my father—for so many years the dream lived within me. As life mysteriously sometimes does, circumstances prevented such a move. But the desire—the need—was there. Desperately longing for our home, it was John's music which kept us focused on making the dream a reality, no matter what. John's music fed our spirits and our souls. It gave us hope; I still remember my father's tears as he listened to *To The Wild Country* and *Rocky Mountain High*. That life for us was so far away, but one day—one day—till then, we listened to John sing of the dream within.

That wonderful day came on Thanksgiving 1985, and how our hearts were filled with gratitude as we moved into our mountain cabin surrounded by 14,000-foot-peaks. The entire trip out to Colorado, we played tape after tape of John, as we made our dream come true, driving the miles to our real life of freedom, peace, and solitude amongst the mountain wilderness we had yearned for so long.

John's music and his many humanitarian activities became an even stronger influence. For now, I had become an adult, capable of really implementing the things he was encouraging us all to do: to get involved and make a difference for good in this world. That message became a part of me, and it's that message I want to share.

Never in my life have I experienced such pain as when I learned of John's death. Grief like this I never knew. I had lost a brother. It's something I'm sure many of you felt—the deepest pain which seemed unbearable. I've never cried as I have for John.

Solace was sometimes found in knowing John would want us to still find joy in life, to celebrate his life, and continue the dream. Yet, there remains a deep inner yearning to be able to say to him, "Thank you, John. Thank you for everything." I believe that all of us who feel this way will one day have that opportunity to again express how much he meant to us.

And yet that pain still surfaces. My mind fills with those unanswerable questions. Why? Where was divine protection? Why? He was so good; a light for us all. Why?

Then my heart turns to my favorite songs where so many truths are found. "Living and dying are both our most intimate friends," he sang in *Zachary and Jennifer.*

"My body is merely the shell of my soul... my spirit will never be broken nor caught... for the soul is a free flying thing," in *Eagles and Horses.*

Though I truly believe that as eagles fly free, John also is soaring, finally home and free from the burdensome constraints of this world, I can't help but wonder, as in *On The Wings of a Dream*, "why is it thus we are here, and so soon we are gone?"

For the longest time I wondered if I'd ever "fly again," his loss overwhelmed me and my usual optimism and hope in life. But I've found it again, and it is my deepest hope that you do also. To love those in our lives so completely—to love all—every stranger, far or near, as our brother and sister—to love Earth—only then do we fly. Only then do we manifest, in our lives, what John did in his life.

It is here we must begin. Each of us can make a difference; that was John's message time and time again. I'm still "looking for space," but in finding out who I am, I've realized that easing others' pain and protecting this Earth is essential to becoming all I can and am meant to be. It is the same for each of us.

Although there are times of darkness, of deep sadness and discouragement, I come back to the understanding that it is only we who love, who will make a difference and change the sad situations in life for our family of man and the Earth. I always return to the same dream John had of peace and love. What is vital is that each of us continues the dream he had: a world of peace; a world of abundance; a world where none of us lack that which we need.

I write this for others who, like me, sometimes find themselves surrounded by a world full of "sadness and screams" (*Looking for Space*), who feel themselves alone in this often cold universe. We are not alone. It is this of which we can be sure. There are others, like you, who wish to continue John's dream. Together, we can make it happen.

Toward that, I urge you to become involved with some of the wonderful causes John believed in. Channel our energies into every relationship we have: with friends, family, or partners. Never forget the most important thing we can do on Earth is to love one another. It is the answer. No matter where we are, there are opportunities to make a difference in others' lives. Every single action we take is part of the whole.

As John so perfectly expresses in *Wandering Soul:* "Love is the answer, and love is the way... Love is knowing just what to do and what to say."

John was a beautiful man; a man who believed in love and wanted to teach others the same. He was our teacher—and now we must continue that vision—and we must teach others.

I believe John is home now, in perfect freedom his spirit sings and soars, and I believe he is here for us, still speaking to our hearts, still guiding and inspiring, all we have to do is listen and he will be there for every receptive heart. As he said in *On The Wings of a Dream*, "In a smile or a tear... Or a prayer or a sigh or a song." John was and is a friend from our heavenly home—we are never alone.

John–Always Flying For Me

It's another beautiful spring in the Colorado Rocky Mountains, blue skies, bright sunshine, cool breezes, and tender green buds interspersed with blooming dandelions greet me each morning. The mountains are graced with glistening snow. Off somewhere a hawk is heard, and as its graceful body soars above, I think of John–flying for me.

Sometimes it's amazing to think about the joy I've again found, that wonderful feeling that life is good, and that there is so much for me yet to do. A sweet happiness is mine once again despite the terrible pain of losing John from this Earth. Despite the tears, I know John wants me to fly. He wants all of us to fly, and the joy which makes that possible comes only when we bring love to everything we do each day. Miraculously, love given to others eases pain–theirs and ours.

John spent his life flying, literally and metaphorically. Surely the sensation of piloting those planes was wonderful; seeing all he could see. But John also knew the pleasure of flying while his feet were firmly on the ground. His spirit flew as he knew the freedom and joy of sharing. He knew and taught us that it's only when we love that we fly. Despite the pain of living in this realm, we are meant to love–we are meant to fly.

Easter has recently passed with its story of a man who loved, gave his life, and has risen–a story reminiscent of all great teachers of love who have come and gone. Their short time upon this Earth left behind a legacy of such magnitude that we will always recognize and celebrate that they came to show us the way. I think of Jesus, Gandhi, Buddha–I think of John. In both ancient and modern times there have been souls who have recognized the necessity of love and lived their lives in an effort to teach that truth to others.

Such souls experience many tribulations and much pain during their human existence, yet somehow they cope with the pain of suffering and maintain that love is the answer to it all.

John suffered in his life–that's obvious. We all suffer. But he maintained his faith in purpose and his trust in love. Thus, as we know, he worked in so many ways to help, inspire, and ease other people's pain, in spite of the pains he went through.

It takes strength to work for peace when you're enduring great emotional pain. It takes courage to commit your life to relieving others' suffering when you find yourself in despair. Very few have such strength and courage—but John did. He flew—he is flying now.

So it is with each of us. We are born, grow, experience sadness and joy, feel pain and happiness, and—if we choose, as John did, we can fly—for ourselves and for others.

John's beautiful memorial song, *Flying for Me*, expresses a deep appreciation for the *Challenger* crew. But it also communicates his heart's desire to "give a voice to all of the hearts that cannot be heard, and for all of the ones who live in fear." Here, again, we find John's love for others. Poignantly he sings, "I wanted to give myself and free myself, and join myself with it all." He has.

As he intended, it is a wonderful tribute to the space shuttle crew, but it is also something more—an exceptionally personal ballad of John's essence: his dreams, his vision for a better world, his hope that his life would contribute to the welfare of others.

I often find myself thinking of John's life and death. John gave us his light, he gave us his spirit and all he could be. And to me, *Flying for Me* is really a tribute to each soul who lives life from love—from a wanting deep within to be part of the movement—part of the growing—part of the difference.

Believing in love will not protect us from pain, sadness, or sorrow... in fact, I think we'll have more of it in our lives. But that's not a bad thing. It is, as John sings, part of life. To refuse to acknowledge it is to refuse part of life. Being in touch with our innermost feelings is essential to being able to express love in the fullest way—and to all.

I believe John's hope for each of us, while our spirit is within this human form, is that we fly—that we love all life—that we give love in every breathing moment we have—that we exclude nobody from that love. And that we remember that despite the pain we have while on Earth, life is worth living. For as John said so perfectly, "In the midst of this incredibly insane world with all the terrors and problems, life is worth living. I love life, and everything about it. The first thing that is there for me in every relationship, in every aspect of living, is this celebration."

So, spread your wings. Endeavor to examine your life, to develop ways to express love to all. Make no exceptions—always love. No matter how much pain you feel, no matter what you have done, or what has been done to you, no matter what happens—always love. Then you will, like John, fly.

Seasons of the Heart

Time... seasons... changes... the thoughts and pondering which occupy the heart of a wandering soul are so unlike the thoughts of those who choose a conventional path. For the wandering soul seeks truth, seeks guidance it knows only comes from within and which is nourished, and therefore enhanced, by the experience of silence.

John, our example, struggled between the demands of his career (and its inherent stress) and the time and space he needed to himself. He was "in the world"—but not "of the world" for a purpose, which despite the difficulties, he knew was part of the greater good. John's music was an expression of all seasons of his heart, not merely a vehicle for entertainment. His music contains power to strengthen and inspire because it is from the inner voice of truth, the voice there for each of us, if we listen.

To choose to relate to this insane world always brings one degree or another of hell into our lives. But we do it because, like John, we believe our involvement is necessary to ease some of the suffering we see. As John certainly experienced, fighting for good—for peace—brings with it the realization we will have to contend with formidable enemies of the truth, enemies who will do everything in their power to stop us. But the light within will shine forever, leading us through the darkness into the purpose which has been set for each of us.

Time, as a human measurement, is in itself meaningless, though it, of course, serves as a useful tool for co-ordinating human activities. Sadly, society has come to believe 'time' really exists, and therefore most people cling to the non-existent 'past' and plan for the non-existent 'future' as if these are distinctive states of being.

Those in touch with the Spirit know otherwise. We know it is only this very moment which exists; the 'past' is no longer, though the memory of life experiences endures, and from hence wisdom comes. The 'future' is held in the most careful regard, because we know every action taken now will have an effect. By combining life-experience wisdom with "hope for the future" we can "be all that we can be... not just what we are." (*Rhymes and Reasons*)

Aspiring to live each precious moment of our lives in love fulfills our purpose.

The human measurement of time falls short when contrasted with the heart's time and space—the seasons of the heart. For as John so perfectly expresses in *Around and Around*, "Time as I've known it doesn't take much time to pass by me... minutes into days turn into months turn into years, they hurry by me... still I love to see the sun go down, and the world go around."

For those, like John, who choose love, the human existence passes quickly. For the heart's devotion to loving, to truly living, to embracing the Spirit, to working against injustice, to easing others' pain while enduring our own, appears sometimes as a never-ending task—but a welcome one.

A true life purpose is never-ending. John's purpose is not over, though his human presence upon Earth is. He accomplished tremendous good while here, and although we may ask as John did "why is it thus we are here and so soon we are gone?" (*On the Wings of a Dream*), I believe the answer is in the heart in those moments away from the cares of the world. It's an answer I've come to know in the year and a half following John's death.

Though our minds suggest we want to live forever, our heart, our Spirit, knows better. There is only so much to endure and suffer for the greater purpose. To give our gift, our unique aspect of light, to this world is all we must do—and then in 'time' come home.

But if lived in love, our gift remains and grows through the lives of people we've touched, through our purpose, through our songs, our work for the planet and humanity, our family and friends, the writings we've imparted, the art we've created, through each and every way that something we've done has touched another soul's heart—we live forever.

John lives in the love that lives in your heart. Follow it, it will lead you home. For as far away as he may seem, you are never really apart, as John sang in *Children of the Universe*, "It's in your dreams that you will know the seasons of the heart."

Sunshine and Snow

It's a brisk Saturday morning in the mountains–a typical February day–as I hike the country road, passing over the frozen stream surrounded by brilliant, though barren, aspen and poplar trees, their bark glistening in the sun. Sunshine and snow days–days when I feel a part of everything I see.

It is here I often stop. A small grove overhanging the ice-covered stream; squirrels and birds often liven this spot with their chattering and song, but not in the early morning. Morning finds it silent but for the tinkling of water passing below the frozen layer–water music– which always reminds me of John.

It's a sweet, pure sound sometimes accompanied by the rustle of branches as a breeze comes through. Yet, for all its gentleness as it flows from the high mountains to the spot where I stand, it has an intrinsic strength. This water, a drop or a torrent, is constant and never-ending. It is life-giving– flowing evermore–like John.

I cannot explain why the water music reminds me so of John. Reflecting upon him happens often, but rarely as it does at the frozen stream–with sunshine and snow.

John often spoke and sang of what many perceive as opposites: joy and sorrow, promise and pain, life and death. He knew the truth. These are not opposing forces. They are one–just as we are. The circle of life encompasses all emotions, all experiences. They are linked.

A few days ago, I met yet another beautiful spirit whose heart is obviously filled with love for John. I have met a good number of such individuals, those who pattern their lives after what he taught us, who see him as the teacher he was, imparting wisdom to those who would listen. It is such people I speak to now, those whose hearts still feel grief. Yes, the days are easier now; "Time is the master of healing," as John sang in *Love is the Master*, and love is truly "the master of everything that we do." But, though healing takes place, there will be times still when you cry. That is good.

I asked my new acquaintance who had influenced her most in life. "John Denver," she replied, explaining to me how in his music, he had amazingly captured her feelings and her thoughts, as if he knew her mind and could perfectly express in song what she had felt throughout her life. Tears came to my friend—and to me.

It is precisely this power of John's music which reaches our hearts. Yet, examining his songs, we see a variety of emotions—some just plain happy, others reflective, others sad. Why? Because he always sang of life—not the illusions society often calls life: he sang of the heart. And within the heart there is no contradiction, although many aspects of true emotion exist.

I believe we must never deny or try to shut out such true emotion, regardless of what it concerns: family, career, relationship, or John. Living in light, in truth, we will experience a range of emotions—none bad—not even the darkness. Why do we hurt? Why do we see suffering? Why do we suffer? As John said in *Hold on Tightly*, "Here in the heart are the answers to questions much deeper than these."

I offer this advice to those of you who celebrate John—those who laugh and smile with him—those who shed a tear over him—and who, as he would be happy to see, shed tears for the pain of others. Do not question the validity of the tears, the grief, or despair. For these are manifestations of the beauty, the power, the love within.

Rather, experience them, then turn your heart toward the sun. Realize being in touch with yourself in such a deep manner gives you the power to affect change in this world. There is no contradiction—not in this life—or thereafter.

The essential point we can learn from John's life and death is to live each moment to the fullest. The only way we do that is to love—love all—without exception. Choosing such a path, as John did, will bring us more pain, because love opens our hearts to all experience, and it allows us to experience true joy.

Those of us who truly love John share this: We are dedicated to continuing his legacy. We laugh about him, we cry about him, and therein is our strength. Our passion is not diminished because he has left this physical world.

Some of you have shared with me apologetically that there are days when you are sad–and yet I know you are the same people who work diligently to help others and this Earth.

Those who work for peace and believe in love are perceived as weak by the powers that be. An employer, a government official, a politician, a warden, a family member, or any other in a position of power whose heart is corrupt, will regard those who believe in love and peace as weaklings to be abused.

I implore each of you to not view yourself as they do. The power is with you–John is with you. "Love is the answer," he told us in *Wandering Soul*. But John also said in *It's a Possibility*, "Though the heart is just a lover, it's never afraid to fight."

I emphasize this point to you. Fighting, whatever form it takes, is sometimes a necessity. Peace is not weakness–it is standing for what is truly loving; it is fighting for justice in whatever place we find ourselves. Love is power, but it must be put into action. It is not something that resides within us and never sees the light. We are each a lamp, a vessel, through which the light shines. Never fear expressing yourself. Never fear the repercussions. Take action now. For many of you are right this moment in the midst of a situation which requires it– all of us are, in fact–it's life.

Do not miss the point. We are here to love, no matter what it takes: time, commitment, persecution, stress, or even our lives.

"Some will fill the emptiness inside by giving it all to the things they believe," John tells us in *Higher Ground*. That is exactly the way to fill the void. Yet, I see some "filling it" by denial of their emotions; and I see some turning to others they can "follow"–but I tell you this is not the way.

John was a man, a beautiful spirit. He, as with many other teachers throughout history, had fans or followers. But those people are not the ones who continue the dream. For them, John's physical absence leaves a void they desperately seek to fill with someone else they can follow.

The ones who truly understand John's message do not seek this. Yes, they can appreciate other teachers, but they do not need another. For they know the power of John's message to us lives, and it is this which they believe and are committed to, not the man—but his mission—the lessons he taught us and teaches us. Do not miss the point. We honor and celebrate him by giving ourselves to love.

John's example, John's music, John in Spirit will be with you. But you must make the step to always love, even when it means a battle. The forces of good must, in every situation of life, not turn away. You must speak your mind, do what is right despite the apparent consequences; fight evil directed toward you or toward others or the Earth. You are the possibility of "no more suffering and no more sorrow." (*It's a Possibility*) in the space you have been placed in this lifetime. Changing the world takes each of us doing whatever we can do, right where we are.

We will honor John best by having the courage to truly embrace love, no matter what it requires of us.

In gentleness is strength, not passivity, as a gentle stream becomes a part of the great ocean, never underestimate the power within. It is there, but you must use it.

If you truly love John, then use his life as a guide. He fought hard—and he hurt. He challenged powerful forces of greed, indifference, apathy, destruction—whether they were corporate, political, governmental, or personal, he stood up and fought. Doing so will anger others, but it must be done. Fight injustice wherever you see it—in a small town or a metropolis, in a place of work or in the family. Fight for this Earth, the human family, for life. Never fear standing up for what you believe—fight.

You will truly experience joy—and embrace the Spirit John sang of.

The sun is brightly shining. Warmth hits my face, as the coolness of the mountain breeze captures the cold of the snow around me. Sunshine and snow, I love this, it is perfect, it nourishes me—joy and pain—love and strength—peace and fighting—life and death. No contradiction.

JOHN

BY CHRISTINE MOON

Christine Moon, President of the England-based Friends of John Denver organization operating throughout the United Kingdom, succinctly expresses the gratitude felt by many to John.

His words resonated with the truths that had always lived in my heart. His was the voice of my soul. He reminded me that we all are one, and that we are never alone. He awakened my spirituality, and led me to my true family. He taught me to rejoice in the differences and to remember that as different as we are, we're still the same.

His compassion was boundless. His love for all people and creatures shone like a beacon in the darkness of night. I shared his joy as he walked in the sunshine of life, and felt his pain when clouds gathered. In his darkest hours, he never lost sight of his dream of a brighter future for us all. His courage never failed him as he worked tirelessly in pursuit of that vision.

He was both very special, and very ordinary. As his fame spread across the planet, he never lost his humility. His music and poetry soothed troubled hearts and minds, and his wisdom influenced many positive actions. He showed me what one man can do, and I saw that each of us can make a difference to the future.

Now this beautiful spirit has returned Home, yet a part lives on in each of our hearts. His time among us was an inspiration to us all, and we learned much of great value. Let us share his message with the world, and make our dream of peace and harmony among all people a reality".

HEART TO HEART

Since the writing of the tribute and the memorials, I have received thousands of letters from people all over the world whose lives were touched by John. There are those who feel they survived cancer, brain tumors, grand mal epilepsy, or heart failure, because of the message they received in his music. There are those who contemplated suicide because of extreme emotional or physical trauma, and again it was John's music that pulled them through.

These people share two things: their lives were wondrously affected by John (often literally saved), and their hearts still longed desperately to express to John their appreciation.

Not everyone was able to have the opportunity to hold John's hand, look him in the eyes, and say "Thank you". Many letters came from people who yearned to do this. Some had fallen into the trap of guilt, but John believed in the relinquishment of guilt. All that matters is that we learn and grow. No guilt should exist for the fact we were unable to thank him. If your spirit shines because of what you learned from him, all you must do is speak to him. He will hear, for in the Spirit, all things are possible.

Here are excerpts from some of the most poignantly touching letters. This book would not be complete without giving representational voice to the millions out there who loved John.

"Life is so short... wish we could have all met John... maybe you did personally... but in spirit we all did. I've never known someone or cared about someone the way I do for John. He's given me a voice when I was hurting and couldn't find comfort."—a letter from North Carolina

"It seems that all of John's songs really carry a special message, at least to me. This one [Whispering Jesse] tells me to cherish the one I love, to do something special for him every day. Sometimes it is doing an errand for him, and other times it is saying a simple prayer, that God will guide him through this day and keep him safe. Again, I want to say 'thank you,' John, for your simple message of peace and love. May we all learn to live it and share it, and the world will be much better than when we first found it."—a letter from Illinois

"I was a 'late comer' to John's music... I am now 53 years of age, but I didn't find John till 1982, when, watching a released British concert of John's, at Christmas time, [I] became enthralled with this guy—whose pure voice, gentle manner and honesty took my heart there and then! This guy was saying things that I wanted to feel, to do, to stand up for. Ever since that magic evening I never stopped loving John."—a letter from England

"Although I have 'known' you [John] only for five years, I cannot imagine what my life would be like without you. To think that my eighth grade algebra teacher would introduce me to you! But I am so grateful he did, for you have opened my eyes to a whole new world I never knew existed—a world where people aren't cruel; a world where the sun shines; a world where you can 'celebrate living—everyday.' ... When I reach the point when it seems as nothing I do matters, that I will never help to show people why our Mother Earth needs our help, I think of you, all you accomplished, and how, in the end, you didn't give up. Even though you are not with me physically, and even though I can't see you or touch you, I can hear you: in my dreams, in your songs, in my actions, and in the stillness of the day... You help me to calm my emotions down when they become almost unbearable. You're there for me through thick and thin, through the good times and the bad times. When I begin to think my mind is playing tricks on me and that I'm really NOT sensing your entity, I just remind myself the afterlife is something the mortal mind just can't possibly imagine, that after you die your Spirit flows freely from one place to another, and then I believe you are there... How can I continue your legacy? How can I carry on in your footsteps and 'make the world a better place?' How can I find peace, happiness, and serenity? Am I making the right choices? All of these questions and so many more haunt my days and nights. But knowing you will be there for me to help me through these troubled times allows me to feel at least remotely better. I could go on and on

about what you have done for me and how much you mean to me...
Please never forget me; I know that I will never forget you."—a letter
from Georgia

"I'll never forget something John said in *Heart to Heart*. He addresses
this very problem, and he says the answer is simple as 'you and me.' The
opposite is our problem—when we think 'you or me.'"—a letter from
Illinois

"I had my own day of tribute. Actually, every day I put a lot of
attention on John Denver."—a letter from Washington state

"Gone was my headache, gone was the desire to take an overdose and
end my life. Thank you, John, and thank you, God, for sending John
Denver and his wonderful music into my life."—a letter from Illinois

"I guess I latched on to John's music in the mid 70's when my wife
decided to go 'off and find herself,' leaving me with two of our three
boys. The positive aspects of that incident were that we did more things
together and became a tighter family unit. We started skiing together,
got in touch with John's music, headed out to Colorado for a spring ski
trip each year (from our home in Wisconsin), and started attending
John's concerts whenever they were held in Milwaukee or Chicago. We
attended them all and I can remember sitting near the back row of the
old basketball sports stadium on the west side of Chicago, but because
of John's ability to react with everyone of the thousands in attendance,
we might as well have been in the front row."—a letter from Colorado

"I thrived on what John is about."—a letter from New Zealand

"I love all kinds of music, but there's something about that voice that
touches me like no other. I wish I could explain it. It gets under the skin
and somehow into the soul. It was truly a gift he was given to be able
to reach people that way. I've never known anyone else with that same
kind of magic."—a letter from New York

"You cannot miss the many references he makes to a Higher Power,
especially the One who created the world and the environment that he
so revered! ... I could watch John grow and mature, and as he searched
for the 'meaning of life'—Why we are here? What is our purpose of
being?—and I'm trying to answer these questions in my own life.

Obviously I have very few answers, but I do have to say he has changed some of my ways of thinking... it's almost impossible to explain why this one person's 'gift' has so affected my life."—a letter from Indiana

"That evening [Valley Forge Concert, 1996] changed my life forever. John's voice was beyond beautiful, especially on Oh, Holy Night. *His stage presence was almost an enigma. On one level, he seemed so immediate, so connected to the audience; on another, he seemed to be in a higher place, one very few reach. In retrospect, I feel he was already partly gone from us... John's influence on me is huge, even though I'm his contemporary. He opened my eyes, my ears, my mind and my heart. I'll never be the same... I haven't grieved anything like this for my father, grandmother, aunt, close friends who've died. I never knew John, yet I shed tears all the time for him. What is it about this man?"—a letter from Pennsylvania*

"I always wanted to be able to meet him, but felt I 'knew' him any way through his songs and concerts and his explaining why and how he came about writing a certain song."—a letter from Florida

"[regarding finding friends who also love John] I put this all down to John still weaving his spell. It has opened up a new life for me, and there is so much I want to do to carry on his work... My children are married, with their own families, and times have been very lonely... I love music, reading and nature, now I have found souls who don't think I am mad to worship the memory of John. It's something I have kept quiet about in the past, for fear of being looked at as though I was mad."—a letter from England

"He really has the best fans in the world that care about him more than ever. We still follow him as he says in his song... I wish more people understood John the way some of us do... what he was all about."—a letter from New Jersey

"In April 1997, my husband and I were thrilled to find out I was pregnant with our second child. I had just seen John in concert in February of that year. Four weeks later, my beloved grandfather died. John and his music helped me get through that difficult time... I like to say that my son was 'cooked' on John Denver. I played his music loud and constantly for nine months. I decided to make a tape of my favorite songs to listen to during labor. [The early morning of December 7, 1997]

... my labor progressed quite normally. When I started to get really uncomfortable, I asked for a continuous epidural drip, all the while listening to John. At about 3:20 pm, my doctor informed me that I was fully dilated, and it was time to push. At 3:45 pm, to the wonderful sounds of Sweet Surrender, *our son Brendan JOHN was born. He was perfect. Brendan is two now and still listening to John's music. I KNOW John is Brendan's guardian angel, he sings him to sleep every night. I have felt his presence from day one. He was with me in the labor/delivery room and he is with me still."—a letter from Pennsylvania*

"I'm so truly grateful to John for his legacy of care, love and such wonderful music—I couldn't cope without him."—a letter from England

"John is very much with us, perhaps in ways we do not always realize. Hardly a day goes by that I don't think of him."—a letter from Illinois

"I miss him. John was truly blessed with a gift directly from the hand of God. I wonder how many people really look at the world as he did; if they did, this might be a nicer place to be... He was an amazing man... John had a appreciation for the truly complex world we live in and how everything has a purpose and the balance isn't ours to tamper with... I never write these things but somehow needed to say it."—a letter from California

"JD won't attain any more ages than 53, but in some ways he has become ageless because his followers are intent on cherishing his memory and passing down his music to future generations. JD gives us boomers a prophet of peace."—a letter from Texas

"On October 12, as every year since John Denver was killed, we traveled to the Big Horns. We go to the two places we found that awful October to think of this great man who played such an important part in our lives...We have not seen the two eagles there since that first October, but their presence is always remembered... that tragic time of our life when they came to comfort us."—a letter from Wyoming

"At times [personal difficulties described] like this, it's easy to lose one's perspective—but John's words help me through."—a letter from England

"As a young child growing up in the Highlands of Scotland I was always surrounded by music... My mother's parents—now sadly both no longer alive—were my Grandad Alex and my Granny Annie who enjoyed nothing more than having their grandchildren over. One early evening I recall helping set the dinner table, when I stopped in my tracks and listened to the song being played on the record player and asked my Grandad what song was playing. He looked on the play list of an Irish flute player, James Galway, and wittily remarked "Oh, that's Granny's Song!" I was unsure what he was meaning by that, so I looked when his back was turned and saw the correct title was *Annie's Song*... For almost 20 years as a John Denver fan, my birthday/Christmas gifts always included his music. I had always hoped one day to be able to meet him, just to offer him my hand in friendship and tell him simply "Thanks." It was a dream I was still hoping [would] come true when I learned the news of his sudden death in a plane accident. John Denver's death hit me hard, like a family member... For almost a year I was 'lost,' alone with just my thoughts and music. I believe that fate however has brought me a new John Denver family... John Denver's music and spirit has given me so much joy during the last 20 years, I am now very proud to know and help people continuing his legacy... As long as they continue their message of hope under John's name in written word and his music, his spirit will always be alive."—a letter from Scotland

"Life has never quite been the same knowing that John is no longer here to share his thoughts and his music with us... I think you would understand when I say that I often talk to John—sometimes laugh with him—still cry with and for him. But I guess it has been this belief that there really is still John's presence with us that has kept me going."—a letter from England

"John Denver's isn't the only music that moves me, but it's the BEST. He is the epitome of the spirit of the earth, of nature, of that special healing vibration."—a letter from Washington state

"Too little has been done to honor this great man."—a letter from New York

"During this painful time [after losing a job], I found the song *Looking for Space* was a huge comfort to me as the words fitted my situation exactly. In the end, I came out into 'the sunshine and my dreams' as I found a job as a teacher's aide within 3 weeks of the other job. I am still there and enjoying it immensely, especially the feeling that I can make a difference to the children's lives by helping them. John's words were so true to what was happening in my life that it was as if he had written the song especially for me."–a letter from England

"Here is one more person who was (and is) lifted and thrilled by the voice of John Denver... Wherever we are, whatever we do, his voice adds much to our lives. His death is the loss of a loved one. He will always be a special friend."–a letter from Idaho

"[After arriving home on Sunday, October 12, 1997, during heavy rain at 1700 German time] As we had arrived at home, everyone jumped into the house; I was last, with some bags. Before I closed the front door, I turned around to look outside once more (why?). And I saw the rainbow; the two rainbows in the sky; the sky is deep blue; in a way I have never seen before–the rainbow colors so intense. I put down my bags immediately and looked. It amazed me. And suddenly "Paint us a rainbow without any end" was on my mind. I wrapped my arms around me, there was a very strange feeling, I did not know why. [This lady immediately took a photo of the rainbow as she was so awe struck by its brilliance and by the foreboding she felt. The following day she read of John's death on the videotext and later calculated the time difference. She had seen the rainbow within minutes of his plane crash.] But above all, for me I know, this double rainbow belongs to JD... an adios. It must be a promise."–a letter from Germany

"How can I miss him so much when I never even knew him? I really do feel like he is my best friend. He is always here for me when I'm sad and depressed."–a letter from Minnesota

"[En route from Indonesia to Aspen to attend memorial for John Denver] a wonderful thing happened to me in LA at the airport... walking from the International Arrival terminal to American/Continental terminal, there was a lady sitting all alone in a wheelchair with lots of equipment connected to her. I noticed a suitcase was turned over in front of her, so I leaned over to pick it up for her. I smiled and spoke and started to walk on. She made a small movement with her hand so I leaned over to listen. Her oxygen breathing tube had fallen out and she needed me to put it back in her mouth. I was really worried about her being alone, so decided to spend some time with her.

Someone had gone to get the van for her. I did most of the talking because it seemed very difficult for her. She did want to know why I was there, where I was going. I started to tell her about the special reason I was going to Aspen. She got the most beautiful smile on her face and whispered, 'I should have known you are one of John's own.' That was the nicest thing I have had said to me in many years... It took one minute or less to lean over and pick up that suitcase. I think about what would have happened if I had ignored her like everyone else. I have no idea about the oxygen and whether she would have gone into some kind of distress. It meant a lot to her, but not half as much as it meant to me." a letter from Texas

"For my fiftieth birthday in '98, I was going [to go] to a concert anywhere in the United States. Raising kids and teaching just didn't allow me the time for such things. Now, it is one of the greatest regrets of my life."—a letter from Indiana

"The year my mum passed away and I lost one of my best friends to cancer and had major bowel surgery, I wore out *Different Directions,* particularly playing *Tenderly Calling* and *Foxfire Suite.* As a counselor at an Easter Seals Camp, I hand-wrote 20 copies of *Looking for Space* to my little charges, who had very severe multiple disabilities. I hoped they took that wisdom of the song and would see not only were they trying to find themselves but so was everyone else... and Sweet Surrender showed me how to look at the simple abundance in the world... learning how to go with the flow, surrendering yourself to the experience of life and living and reveling in that experience. John gave me inspiration all through my life and despite his untimely passing, continues to do so."—a letter from Canada

"John was such a treasure, such a gift to the world."—a letter from North Carolina

"I can't find the words to say how much John's words, music, and his compassion and love mean to me. On good days, I find inspiration in his life and on bad days I find comfort in listening to him sing."—a letter from England

"As with so many people, I feel I would not be who I am without John's incredible influence. I am 41 and always feel like I am not getting older, just wiser because of his music."—a letter from Oklahoma

"I listen to his music and my soul fills up with satisfaction, love for life and people, and such peace that I never felt before with any other music. John wrote and sung with his soul bared, his songs just lift my spirit with every single word and note... I appreciate more every little thing around me, and that feeling is growing more and more every day. I have even had moments when I start singing in my mind one of JD's songs, and suddenly everything around me seems to change for the better. It's kind of surreal sometimes... You can sense it in his voice, it's like he tried to tell us all the time that life is worth living and that the simple things he sang about—love, friendship, nature—those are the things that really matter."—a letter from Puerto Rico

"I love John dearly—always have and always will. I guess we are all a soul family, I'm sure we will be reunited with John in another lifetime (as we have known him in previous lives)."—a letter from England

"I grew up with John Denver's music, but just as he said his music took on new meaning for him as he got older, I have found that his music has taken on all new meanings for me, too. As we mature, we realize more and more the importance of loving one another, working in harmony, respecting the Earth and all that live here. Who else but John Denver communicated that message more clearly, effectively and passionately! Even now, after all this time, he has helped me to grow. And now my 14-year-old son has discovered his music, and he too looks at the world with more concern, and love and respect. I hope John feels our gratitude and love—wherever he is."—a letter (locale unknown)

ACKNOWLEDGEMENTS

It is with deep gratitude I wish to thank my good friend Debra Chilton—for the things we share and the work we do together for peace. And my appreciation goes to Jennifer Carmody, Rob Clark, Tess Farrington, Jean Kendle, Dan King, Kathy Lill, Margaret Moores, Morgan and Charles Sanderson, Melinda Tanner, and Melanie Trondson. And a thank you to my other friends worldwide whom I have met because of John. It would be impossible to name you all. I am pleased you have shared of your lives with me. I thank all of you for believing in the power of John's music and being part of the humanitarian work I do—and for being friends.

A warm expression of gratitude to my photographers: Dreux DeMack of Tulsa, Oklahoma; Inge Kaminski of Dusseldorf, Germany; and Christine Moon of Leicester, England. The three of you love John. I am happy you have shared your memories of John with others through the photographs in my book. Also, I am grateful to Dr. Bette Loiselle, Director of the International Center for Tropical Ecology (University of Missouri-St. Louis) for providing the photograph of John receiving his ICTE World Ecology Medal. My dear friend Christine Richardson took the portrait photo of myself.

I also wish to thank those who assisted my research with information and interviews: Debra Chilton; Chuck Woolery, Issues Advocacy Director of the World Federalist Association; Aaron M. Knight, Chief of Staff, World Federalist Association; Kris O'Connor; Tom Poberezny; and Lorraine Smith. Also, my appreciation to those who interviewed John in the past, who are acknowledged throughout this text, as well as to Cherry Mountain Music and Dreamworks Songs of Cherry Lane Publishing, the publishers of John's songs for many years.

For all who have walked with me by my side or way back home...

Bless you.

ABOUT THE AUTHOR

Christine Smith is a professional writer, environmental and social justice activist, and Founder/President of the nationwide 501c3 nonprofit Dreams of Freedom, Inc. (an organization which brings the music and videos of John Denver, hygiene items, toys, clothing, and other humanitarian help to prison inmates and their families, as well as to Native American reservations, nursing homes and other places where people need hope and encouragement); it also publishes and distributes an interactive newsletter exploring topics of peace.

Christine works full-time writing feature articles for national and international magazines. These cover a wide range of topics: art, business, psychology, health, environment, social justice, human spirituality, and feature profile interviews with high achievers in many fields.

In addition to her writing, she dedicates her life to continuing John Denver's legacy: she has written memorials and international tributes; co-hosted two 3-hour long radio tributes; appeared as a guest on interview shows regarding him. She hosts the annual John Denver Celebration held in Colorado; sings his songs publicly (including at the yearly celebration); and was Co-Director of the One World John Denver Memorial Peace Cloth presented at the United Nations on Millennium Peace Day in September 2000. She was recipient of the international 2000 Peacepower Amigas Award (from the Women's Peacepower Foundation) in recognition of her "selfless, passionate" activism promoting peace for women and children.

Her other social activism work finds her working diligently to abolish the death penalty in the United States; she is also involved in efforts to protect the wilderness and way of life found in rural Colorado.

Christine lives in a cabin high in the Colorado Rocky Mountains where she enjoys hiking and backpacking, astronomy, reading, chess, singing, cooking, gardening, and playing guitar. Beginning each day with an early morning hike, she derives her inspiration from the peace and solitude of the mountain living she treasures.

You may write her at:

> Christine Smith, author of A Mountain In The Wind
> c/o Findhorn Press
> P.O. Box 13939
> Tallahassee, FL 32317
> USA

Or you may email Christine at: AMountainInTheWind@yahoo.com

For a complete Findhorn Press catalog, please contact:

Findhorn Press

The Park, Findhorn,	P. O. Box 13939
Forres IV36 3TY	Tallahassee
Scotland, UK	Florida 32317-3939, USA
Tel 01309 690582	Tel (850) 893 2920
freephone 0800-389 9395	toll-free 1-877-390-4425
Fax 01309 690036	Fax (850) 893 3442

e-mail info@findhornpress.com
www.findhornpress.com